DISSENTER
IN THE BAPTIST SOUTHLAND

William Wallace Finlator in action, chairing a public hearing of the North Carolina Advisory Committee to the U.S. Civil Rights Commission in August 1977. (Photo by Images Unlimited, from the collection of G. McLeod Bryan.)

DISSENTER
IN THE BAPTIST SOUTHLAND

Fifty Years
in the Career of William Wallace Finlator

BY

G. McLeod Bryan

MERCER
UNIVERSITY PRESS

ISBN 0-86554-176-0

All books published by Mercer University Press are produced
on acid-free paper that exceeds the minimum standards set by
the National Historical Publications and Records Commission.

Library of Congress Cataloging in Publication Data
Bryan, G. McLeod.
    Dissenter in the Baptist southland.
    "Essays and articles by William Wallace Finlator": p. 185.
    Includes bibliographies and indexes.
    1. Finlator, William Wallace, 1913–
2. Baptists—North Carolina—Clergy—Biography.
3. Southern Baptist Convention—North Carolina—
Clergy—Biography. 4. North Carolina—Biography.
5. Church and social problems—United States. I. Title.
BX6495.F46B78   1985   286'.132'0924 [B]   85-13752
ISBN 0-86554-176-0 (alk. paper)

CONTENTS

To
Honora
Creativity   Excellence   Beauty

A FINLATOR CHRONOLOGY

1913 19 June, born in Louisburg, North Carolina.

1930 Entered Wake Forest College.

1934 Entered Southern Baptist Theological Seminary, Louisville, Kentucky.

1935 31 July, ordained a Baptist preacher.

1937 Began ministry to Pittsboro, Bonlee, and Liberty Baptist churches.

1938 4 May, published first article in *Biblical Recorder*.

1940 15 May, published first "Festus Erasmus" column.

1941 Began ministry to Weldon (NC) Baptist Church.
1 October, married Mary Elizabeth Purvis.

1946 Cofounded and edited *Christian Frontiers*.

1946 Began ministry to the First Baptist Church, Elizabeth City, North Carolina.

1948 25 August, resigned from the board of the Southern Conference of Human Welfare.

1950 Opposed dog racing and gambling at Moyock, North Carolina.

1952 January, published "The Prophetic Ministry" in *Crozer Seminary Quarterly*.

1954 Attended World Council of Churches assembly in Evanston, Illinois.

1955 Publicly supported desegregation order of United States Supreme Court.

1956 Began ministry to Pullen Memorial Baptist Church, Raleigh, North Carolina.

1958 Chided Wake Forest College trustees for their failure to desegregate the institution.

1959 21 October, spoke in support of organized labor during textile workers' strike in Henderson, North Carolina.

1960 27 May, spoke to state labor convention for the first time.

1961 Spoke in support of student sit-ins to desegregate public accommodations.

1962 Presented resolution against capital punishment to the Baptist state convention.

1963 Sent open letter to Senators Sam Ervin and Everett Jordan urging them to support human rights legislation.

1965 Sent open telegram to President Lyndon Johnson opposing the war in Vietnam.

1966 Joined peace marches at the Pentagon.

1967 Presented antiwar resolution to Baptist state convention. Resigned from the national board of Protestants and Other Americans for the Separation of Church and State in protest of its anti-Catholicism.
Wrote Christmas letter to Pullen congregation retreating from his vigorous antiwar campaign.

1968 January, published first article in *Churchman*.

1969 29 October, wrote letter to George Meany challenging AFL-CIO support of the war in Vietnam.

1970 Marched with Coretta King in opposition to death sentence imposed on an eighteen-year-old black woman.

1971 Began serving as chairman of the North Carolina Advisory Committee on Civil Rights.

1973 Published open letter refusing to join Billy Graham's crusade in Raleigh.

1974 Proposed abolishing tax exemption for church property.

1977 25 March, sent open letter to President Jimmy Carter reminding him of historic Baptist concerns for peace and human rights.

November, elected vice-president of newly organized Southerners for Economic Justice.

1978 3 April, challenged Wake Forest University because of the antilabor bias of its Institute of Labor Policy Analysis.

1979 23 March, sent open letter to President Carter on behalf of the North Carolina Advisory Committee on Civil Rights, requesting federal pressure to complete the desegregation of the university system of North Carolina.

1980 Received the Frank Porter Graham Award from the North Carolina Civil Liberties Union.

1981 May, asked to retire by the board of deacons of Pullen Memorial Church.

June, successfully presented a motion opposing "interference in religion by the government and interference in government by religious groups" to the Southern Baptist Convention meeting in Los Angeles.

1982 30 June, retired from Pullen Memorial Church.

1983 31 January, obtained FBI file under the Freedom of Information Act.

Gave Clarence Jordan Lectures at Southern Baptist Theological Seminary.

20 April, testified before the judiciary committee of the United States Senate in opposition to use of public school facilities for religious meetings.

2-8 October, gave lectures at Union Theological Seminary, New York.

Presented Frank Porter Graham Award to Father Charles Milholland on behalf of the North Carolina Civil Liberties Union.

1984 May, joined Baptist Peace Mission to the Soviet Union.

1985 15 January, spoke at the convocation of Southeastern Baptist Theological Seminary.

FOREWORD

Gerald Johnson once wrote that Frank Graham found the Sermon on the Mount to be good social and economic doctrine. So it has been with Bill Finlator, Dr. Frank's companion spirit. That is why McLeod Bryan's first-rate commentary on the fifty years of Bill Finlator's ministry is important reading; these pages record how one man's labor has made a real difference in the lives of migrant workers, labor union members, religious and political dissenters, and you and me.

Bill Finlator has disturbed a good number of citizens, encouraged many, motivated hundreds and made us all more sensitive to our personal obligation to establish a better and more peaceful world. And at all times he has moved among us with dignity, good humor, grace and good will. One's understanding of and appreciation for this turbulent era in American history is enlightened by Dr. Bryan's fair treatment of William Finlator and his time.

6 September 1984

William C. Friday
President
The University of North Carolina System

PREFACE

William Wallace Finlator was and is a preacher surrounded by controversy. A Baptist, and a Southern Baptist at that, he has labeled the largest Protestant denomination in America "provincial and parochial." A North Carolinian all his life, he has nonetheless repeatedly called it "the most repressive state." A Southerner to the end—by birth, by education and by professional service—he has continually exposed the faults of the South to the world. Believing in civil liberties set forth in the Constitution of the United States—he became a vice-president of the American Civil Liberties Union—he could equally defend the Ku Klux Klan and the Unification Church, the Communist Workers Party and the Roman Catholic Church, the American Nazis and the Christian academies in their legal rights.

Bill Finlator became convinced that the Christian Gospel exposes the acculturation of religion and he has, therefore, expected his words to be at cross purposes with popular values and goals. He seems to think that the more the Gospel is argued in the marketplace and in the political forum the more God may break into human history. He preached for twenty-six years to a congregation of liberal, highly educated, professional people, yet Sunday after Sunday his sermons raised eyebrows and disturbed their middle-class complacency. For Finlator, faith in action is essentially and dramatically controversy over radical commitment. Politeness and good manners notwithstanding—he is a paragon of Southern courtesy—Finlator sees Christianity as a *scandal*. It cannot be domesticated and tamed. It cannot be packaged with the American Way.

In spite of his criticisms Finlator is proud of his Baptist heritage and connections, of the "Ole North State" where he has spent his entire life, of the South that he passionately loves, and of his Pullen congregation, which he accepted at the outset with a reduction in salary. To understand Finlator one is obliged to observe him within the setting that both produced him and resisted him.

The patent caricature of Southern religion emphasizes the pejorative accusations of H. L. Mencken: obscurantism, emotionalism, fundamentalism, moralism and antiintellectualism. Certainly the South has produced its share of this kind of religion, influencing the whole nation with its crowded schools for preachers, with its continuing revivalism spearheaded by its Billy Grahams, and with its concentration of media-programmed religion. It has also produced such radical deviants as E. McNeil Poteat, Martin Luther King, Jr., Clarence Jordan, Will Campbell—and W. W. Finlator. These persons are products of the very institutional religion and local congregations that reflect the mores, manners and prejudices of the Southern life Mencken caricatured. All these persons are Baptists. Other major denominations had the advantage of intellectual achievements, strong theological heritages, and ecumenical connections that helped them transcend the region. But Baptists were not only more Southern than Southerners, they chided the rest of the nation for being less American and reinforced their pride by flatly refusing ecumenical ties.

In literary circles it is now generally accepted that the South has produced its own unique view of the world and of the human animal. William Faulkner, Robert Penn Warren, Flannery O'-Connor, Eudora Welty, and Walker Percy all reflect in their writings a continuing commitment to religion as well as deep religious roots. Their lover's quarrel with the South issues in a profound religious concern that challenges the region's popular religion. If such genius appears occasionally in the South's poets and novelists, may it not also crop up in its pulpits? Finlator seems to be one such example. From the very seedbed of his culture's backwardness and impoverishment, deprivation and struggle, defeat and suffering, he wrested spiritual greatness. Quoting Robert Frost's lines, he himself attributed this to "taking the path less traveled," but there must have been also hidden resources in the seedbed. In writing this survey of Finlator's social activism, I have been guided by two maxims. First, to measure the stature of a great man one must know the proportions of what he is up against. Second, the best history of the times may be found in the sermons of its greatest preacher.

In this book I shall examine Finlator battling for political responsibility and civil liberties, fighting racism, championing the underdog and lost causes, needling the Baptist denomination, cultivating the press and promoting labor unions, working for peace, and trying to fit himself into paradoxical roles—sometimes a prophet, sometimes a humanist. Since this book is no biography, I have not attempted an overall portrait presenting genealogy and childhood, family life and ministerial assignments, or sports and hobbies. However, if one concludes that Finlator's vocation was social agitation and that he exhausted his energies in the excitement of such multifarious adventures, one would not be far from the truth.

Finlator has enjoyed the excitement of the contest, and like Luther he feels that a Christian is measured precisely by how closely he sticks to the thick of the battle. And like the biblical prophets, he seems to have measured his faithfulness by never quitting. He could agree with John Calvin, who wrote that "certainly it was the purpose of God to send forth his servant to various combats, inspired with the confidence resulting from so great a victory, lest he should afterwards be tempted to vacillate." There has been very little vacillation in Bill Finlator; on the contrary he seems to have possessed an overdose of courage. His peculiar paraphrase of the Gospel reads, "There is more sorrow in heaven over one dissenter squelched than over all the antidissident con-

G. McLeod Bryan

servatives safely in the fold." For the five decades between the
1930s and the 1980s, W. W. Finlator has been a voice of dissent
in the South, a dissent planted squarely in the Christian faith.

ACKNOWLEDGMENTS

In thanking the people and institutions who have helped make this book possible, I must first offer my appreciation to the Wisconsin Historical Society, which supplied a microfilm copy of its privileged collection of Finlator papers, and to the Wake Forest University Library Baptist Collection and the North Carolina Archives Department. Second, I am especially grateful to all those persons who have written hundreds of letters to me about W. W. Finlator, sharing stories and personal encounters.

Most of all, I am grateful for the full cooperation of the subject of this study, who not once prevented me from imposing on his time and privacy and who permitted me to probe into every nook and cranny of his public career. Even when I challenged or criticized some of his actions and positions, he never made any attempt to alter the final version or to shape it more favorably to himself. He scrutinized the research at every stage and reviewed carefully every draft of the manuscript to guarantee the accuracy of the facts. He has endeavored to recollect his impressions of certain events and to provide commentary on them in his own words. Wherever in this book no source is ascribed to the quoted words of W. W. Finlator, these quotations come from my interviews with Finlator, and he has approved my transcriptions.

Chapter One

DEVELOPING A POLITICAL THEOLOGY

ADDRESSING THE STUDENTS of Union Seminary, New York, in the fall of 1983, W. W. Finlator confessed, "When I was your age I was a religious traditionalist; in short, a conservative." He was describing his state of mind nearly fifty years earlier. Subsequently he had become known as one of the nation's leading "liberal" preachers, distinguished for his political theology and known as something of a social radical among Southern Baptists. In this chapter, I shall attempt to penetrate the mystery of his metamorphosis, to indicate the sources that impelled his emergence, and to outline the general shape of the political theology he developed.

When Finlator entered college in 1930, the "Social Gospel" had already reached its apogee and was waning. When he retired in 1982, "Liberation Theology" was flourishing. Within the span of those fifty years sandwiched between these two theologies, Finlator had endeavored to formulate his own political theology.

Southern Baptists had, for the most part, neither caught up with the Social Gospel stage nor bothered to interest themselves in the new theology of liberation. Finlator received little assistance from his own household of faith. The Southern Baptist culture in which he grew up was largely "low church," artistically denuded, shoebox housed, evangelical and biblicist, and morally accommodated to white Southern culture. It was also a people's church, fiercely protective of its local autonomy and its lay leadership. "The Southern Baptist Convention," Marshall Frady wrote in 1967,

> has had the effect of reflecting and confirming local prejudices rather than challenging them. . . . [It] exists as the church of the white South. . . . Here in the South the moral challenge of the post-1954 civil rights movement was mounted—and here it was for the most part ignored, sidestepped and in some cases opposed by the churches of the Southern Baptist Convention, the nation's largest Protestant denomination.[1]

Even so, the overall characteristics of the denomination had considerably improved by the time of Frady's description as compared to the church of Finlator's youth, when he was growing up in Raleigh, North Carolina. Southern Baptists of Finlator's youth did possess two saving qualities. First, their memory was obsessed with their radical heritage, both in the Anabaptist tradition of the Reformation and in the dissenting Baptists of the English reformation of the seventeenth century. Second, they had a few outstanding leaders who had become recognized as biblical scholars and who dared apply the Gospel to social issues of the day.

A few Southern Baptist leaders actually embraced the Social Gospel and sought to introduce its message to the Southern Baptist Convention at the state and regional levels. One of these, E. McNeil Poteat, was a pastor in Raleigh at the Pullen Memorial Baptist Church. When its new sanctuary was built, in 1950, he secured America's foremost "liberal" preacher, Harry Emerson Fosdick, for the dedication. But the young Finlator was a mem-

---

[1]Marshall Frady, "God and Man in the South," *Atlantic Monthly* 219 (January 1967): 37.

ber of Tabernacle Baptist Church, where he had been baptized as a boy and was to be ordained at age twenty-two on 31 July 1935. Any creative theological ferment seems to have passed beyond his ken. He recalls having heard the phrase "social gospel" once while a student at Wake Forest College, the leading Baptist college of the state, but if it registered on his mind enough to alter his course of studies, there is no indication. While attending Southern Baptist Theological Seminary in Louisville, Kentucky, he heard it once again. Professor W. O. Carver asked his large class how many knew the name Walter Rauschenbusch; not one person raised his hand

These two instances eloquently attest to the deprivation of Finlator's theological exposure. For the Social Gospel had stirred American Protestantism from 1875 to 1930, and was the subject of major controversies within Protestantism when Finlator was training in the 1920s and 1930s. Fundamentalism contested with the Social Gospel, and biblical literalists battled with liberals for control of local churches. Rauschenbusch, the great prophet of the Social Gospel, had died in 1918, but his many champions, including Professors Harry Ward of Union Seminary in New York City and Jerome Davis at Yale, were advocating his views for the next two decades. Nearer at hand was the open-minded president of Wake Forest from 1905 to 1927, William Louis Poteat. Poteat was professionally a biologist who had pioneered the laboratory method south of the Mason-Dixon line and who had fought the fundamentalists over evolution in the 1920s. He was also a lay theologian strongly embracing the Social Gospel. As early as 1904, he had been instrumental in organizing the Baptist World Congress, an intellectual forum composed of select Baptists throughout the Western world. Through its planning committees and its formal sessions the Congress had welcomed Rauschenbusch's ideas. Rauschenbusch, also a Baptist, was another of its organizers. Poteat's speeches and books (five between 1901 and 1926) consistently expounded the main tenets of the Social Gospel. Poteat helped establish the Christian Social Service Committee within both the Southern Baptist Convention and the State convention. Poteat, Finlator admits, left a deep impression on his college days but not enough to change his course at that stage.

Eastern North Carolina, where Finlator has spent his entire life, was heavily populated with Baptists who retained vivid memories of their radical European beginnings. Theirs was "a trail of blood" shed in opposition to the official churches in Europe, but in the beginnings of America things were little better for them. As an unwanted minority they eked out an existence on the edges of the colonial establishment. The colonial governor, of North Carolina, Lord Tryon, residing in New Bern after coming to office in 1765, regarded Baptist preachers as "rascally fellows," not to be tolerated, and the upstart Regulators as a "faction of Quakers and Baptists." A Baptist preacher, as a delegate to the Constitutional Congress meeting in Halifax in 1776, was responsible for presenting Article 19 of the Bill of Rights, "That all men have a natural and inevitable right to worship Almighty God according to the dictates of their own conscience." Baptist principles on such matters as freedom of conscience, separation of church and state, and democracy in both church polity and secular government were cherished in Eastern North Carolina. When, in 1832, these Baptists moved to establish their own college, they were announcing their arrival into the mainstream. Yet the institution's charter managed to get through the State Assembly by only one vote

The authentic Baptist tradition had come to America by way of a lawyer trained under the celebrated jurist, Edward Coke. This lawyer, Roger Williams, and a doctor, John Clarke, discovered promptly that they were no more welcome in Puritan "New" England than they were back home. Their professional privilege was no protection for them when practicing their radical free church views. Down Virginia way, the Anglicans, even with their broad church doctrine, could not stomach freedom of religion—each county authorized only one free church preacher. Since Baptists were given to multiple lay preachers and to preaching at random without a church house, they found the Anglican establishment too confining, claiming on one occasion that it was more favorable to "Rome than to true Christians." John Ireland and other Baptists went to jail for violating colonial restrictions on preaching and worship.

This Baptist tradition honored radical dissent, independence of mind, and the private conscience. It viewed the Bible as the sole rule of faith, available to "every boy that followeth the plough." John Bunyan, a tinker by trade, was just such a Baptist, and his political stance landed him in jail for a lengthy period where he was able, despite his unschooled background, to produce the masterpiece of the times, *Pilgrim's Progress*. Baptists abhorred war with its massive violence and its tendency to crusade for a pretended Christian nation. The state for them was a secular affair, neutral in morals and religion. Originally they celebrated no state marriage vows, no official holy days (not even Christmas), and they felt that religion must not be mixed with public education. These early Baptists, from the ranks of the artisans, laborers and servants, were ready to usher in God's new age. Bunyan announced in 1658 that "God's own are most commonly of the poorer sort. . . . More servants than masters, more tenants than landlords, will inherit the kingdom of heaven."

As Finlator gradually broadened his concerns, he felt duty-bound to recall his fellow Baptists to their noble origins. When he became editor of an unofficial journal, *Christian Frontiers*, founded by a few Baptists in the South with this purpose in mind, Finlator announced in an editorial in April 1946, "Will anyone deny that this function is to turn the world upside down until the kingdoms of this world become the kingdoms of our Lord?" In a letter to a native of Eastern North Carolina, on 10 October 1973, he confessed, "So few of us Baptists understand our own great principles." Preparing his denomination for the nation's bicentennial, he introduced a resolution to its state convention on 7 November 1974.

> Whereas, we Baptist people, in summoning up remembrance of things past, recall the dungeon, fire and sword our fathers suffered for the faith at the hands of both Protestant and Catholic governments in the old countries, and
>
> Whereas, we also recall the disabilities, harassments and imprisonments to which our forebears in early America were subjected at the hands of the colonial authorities for the civil offense of preaching the Gospel, and

> Whereas, we further recall the vital contribution our Baptist leaders made in forging the American Constitution, and especially its Bill of Rights, guaranteeing religious and political liberties and church-state separation.

Few Baptists in the South were as apprehensive as Finlator about the denomination's increasing neglect of its original ideals and purposes. In 1964 he warned of "the bad image of Baptists."

> We have lived for a long while with the not unfriendly taunt made by other Christian bodies that we are the "problem child of American Protestantism," countering sometimes that we have a peculiar witness to make and at other times replying that after all we aren't even Protestants! . . . In a world teetering on the brink of the final nuclear holocaust, a world of revolutions and race riots, a world also of wars to eliminate poverty and ignorance and the threat of automated unemployment, a world of growing juvenile crimes and a population exploding far faster than our technical society can cope with, what are our Southern Baptist people doing and saying about it? We are fighting the old battle of evolution and book banning. We are voting to keep Negro students out of our colleges. We are rejecting any involvement in a wider spiritual fellowship. We are telling the world as well as ourselves that we don't believe in alien immersion. And we are deciding in momentous debate that a few non-baptists can't sit on our boards of trustees. I am afraid that all the king's horses and all the king's men on Madison Avenue can't help us very much with this image.[2]

Louder than Finlator's verbal challenges to Baptists were his concrete public actions. By the time of this indictment in 1964, his social concerns had found him in places not usually frequented by a white Baptist preacher in the South. He was marching with blacks for civil rights, standing with the opponents of capital punishment, joining the Civil Liberties Union as a charter member, buttonholing lawmakers as legislative chairman for both the North Carolina CLU and the North Carolina Council of Churches, sitting with freedom riders, joining with Martin Lu-

---

[2]W. W. Finlator, "The Baptist Image," *Biblical Recorder* 130 (12 December 1964): 7.

ther King, Jr., in the Montgomery Improvement Association, defending academic freedom, writing newspaper editorials without portfolio, siding with labor against management, promoting unions, fighting censorship, growing uneasy about America's escalating militarism in Southeast Asia, concerning himself with migrant workers, prisoners and Indians, questioning the cold war and unrestrained anticommunism, acting as a United Nations Associate, visiting the White House, and having speeches inserted in the *Congressional Record*. These were but whistle-stops for Finlator on the way to the development of his political theology; he was just picking up steam for the long haul. By 1964 he had completed but a third of his tenure as pastor of Pullen Memorial Church.

Finlator's call to the Pullen Church in 1956 seemed a providential reward for his early steps toward larger social concern. A lawyer who had been a member of Pullen and later of the Elizabeth City church, where Finlator was pastor before coming to Pullen, has described the transition.

> Weldon and Elizabeth City served as good training ground. Those years were a prelude to greater "songs" by [Finlator]. When he reached Pullen he stood on the platform and sang alone in full strength. His "voice" had matured. I remember the last sermon that Bill Finlator preached in the First Church in Elizabeth City. The first half of his sermon was about the Pullen Church and the second half about the Church Universal. I remember thinking then that Bill Finlator was the only man I knew in the whole wide world who would be such a perfect successor to Poteat.

The Pullen Church was indeed the one place in North Carolina that could contain the kind of ministry Finlator had now shaped for himself. Staring him in the face each Sunday was the stained glass window honoring the Baptist radical, Roger Williams. There he inherited the two pet projects of his predecessor: interracial cooperation and an organization called Protestants and Other Americans United. On E. McNeil Poteat's death, Pullen's pulpit committee interviewed Finlator. One of its members told Finlator of the crisis within the congregation over Poteat's advocacy of the 1954 U. S. Supreme Court decision ordering desegregation "with all deliberate speed." But the search committee had written into its job description the assurance of a "free pulpit."

The free and prestigious pulpit of the Pullen Church gave Finlator a platform for the wider ministry he now conceived for himself. There is no denying that he romanticized the Baptist heritage, but by now he was spreading his wings far beyond the Baptist nest. He had deliberately associated himself with movements and persons across the social spectrum who were struggling for a new South. Frank Porter Graham, the outspoken liberal who became president of the University of North Carolina, early became his hero. The organizations Graham promoted became instruments both for Finlator's enlightenment and for his application of the Gospel. Graham, as president of the North Carolina Conference for Social Service, had in 1929 suggested an "Industrial Bill of Rights." In 1938 he headed the Congressional Commission appraising the plight of the South during the depression and producing the report that gave President Roosevelt the slogan, "the South, the nation's Number One Economic Problem." On 6 September 1938 Graham was the keynote speaker instituting the Southern Conference for Human Welfare; Finlator would later become a member of its board of directors.

Besides boosting the National Council of Churches and urging his denomination to affiliate (it adamantly refused), Finlator attended, as an observer, the first American session of the World Council of Churches at Evanston in 1954. He also joined the grassroots ecumenical group devoted to meeting the social needs of the South, the Fellowship of Southern Churchmen, organized in 1936. It brought together such diverse Christian rebels as Charlie Jones of the Chapel Hill Community Church, Howard Kester and Gene Cox of the Tenant Farmers Union, Eugene Smathers of the Friends of the Soil, CIO organizer John Ramsey, Koinonia Farm founder Clarence Jordan, and black professors such as Neal Hughley (Durham), Murray Branch (Atlanta), and Charles Johnson (Nashville). Among the women Finlator encountered in the SCHW were Eleanor Roosevelt and two Southern liberals, Lillian Smith and Lucy Randolph Mason. Benjamin Mays, president of Morehouse College, was a key black influence in Finlator's growth. Mays became vice-president of SCHW, belonged to

FSC, and made the major address condemning racism at the Evanston WCC. He rejected segregation categorically. The same was true of the three women. Eleanor Roosevelt, for instance, defined her grounds at the first session of the SCHW, held in Birmingham, Alabama. She promptly seated herself with the black delegates when Eugene "Bull" Connor, Birmingham's Commissioner of Public Safety, threatened all delegates with jail if they continued to ignore the local Jim Crow laws. Other "liberals" such as Brooks Hays from Arkansas, Francis Pickens Miller from Virginia, and Claude Pepper from Florida all withdrew. They did not want to be identified with "communists and Negrophiles." Finlator was baptized into a new milieu, a larger forum than the Southern Baptist Convention.

Where a person took his final stand, on a concrete issue, became determinative for his future credibility. For instance, Finlator's hero, Frank Graham, backed away from enrolling blacks in his own institution. Pauli Murray's rejection by the University of North Carolina in 1938 became a cause celebre. Howard Odum, the South's leading sociologist, refused to join SCHW but instead founded the more research-oriented Southern Regional Council. Finlator joined that too, but he knew the difference. Gunnar Myrdal's pivotal study of racism, *An American Dilemma,* published in 1944, affected Finlator profoundly. When President Truman's commission issued its report, *To Secure These Rights,* in 1947, Finlator as editor, promptly endorsed it in *Christian Frontiers.*

By the time Finlator became pastor at Pullen he had his fingers in many pies. So it is not surprising that he pushed his congregation in the direction of more ecumenical connections. The church aligned itself with both the American Baptist Convention and the North Carolina Council of Churches. Once its constitution was altered to admit unimmersed Christians Pullen became more like a community church; about fifty percent of the subsequent additions became members without immersion. Yet ecumenism and tolerance became the occasion of Finlator's first controversy within the congregation. His predecessor, Dr. Poteat, had been a founder of Protestant and Other Americans United. Within the congregation were a few members, such as the longtime professor at Meredith College, Dr. L. E. M. Freeman, who cherished Pullen's support of the organization. Finlator, who in his early days had manifested uncritical allegiance to POAU, even to the extent of serving on its national board, now expressed alarm at its overemphasis on anti-Catholicism. He felt a contradiction between welcoming Catholics and Eastern Orthodox communions into the ecumenical movement and constantly questioning their participation in American civic life. In his advocacy of civil liberties he was sensitive to encroachments on the separation principle; in his religious ecumenicity he embraced his Catholic brothers and sisters. Accordingly, he resigned from the POAU board. Some members of Pullen and others thought he had betrayed their cause.

For Finlator, ecumenicity also meant acceptance of Judaism. More and more in his public ministry he found himself working for causes alongside Jews. During the 1967 war he drew up the statement issued by the Raleigh clergy backing Israel. Another time he gave the eulogy for a city rabbi, Leo Stillpass, declaring, "I wish to God that I could be as good a Christian as he was a Hebrew." But, above all, he pleased the Jews in his theology, which accepted the integrity of their faith without seeking to proselytize. In a letter to Professor Bobby Adams of Southwestern Baptist Theological Seminary on 13 July 1981 Finlator explained his position.

> We at Pullen do have a very fine relationship with the Jewish leadership in the community. This has been going on for many years. We have no desire to "convert" any Jew to the Christian faith. We do have a desire to understand how deeply embedded is Christian faith in Judaism. We feel that the more we honor them, the more truly Baptist we will become.

When Finlator saw this relationship tarnished by the remarks of the 1981 president of the Southern Baptist Convention, Bailey Smith—who had made national headlines with the comment, "God Almighty does not hear the prayer of a Jew"—he hastened to renew it. He dispatched an open letter to the rabbis of the three Raleigh synagogues.

> I am always . . . standing in the need of prayer, and I warmly welcome and invite remembrance before the Almighty by the people to whom I am most indebted for my spiritual inheritance. . . . Put me and my fellow Baptists on your prayer list.

The year 1964 may be considered a plateau in the development of Finlator's political theology. For one thing, he had solidly established his own style of ministry within the Pullen church and had earned a reputation for challenging his fellow Baptists to attend to their historic mission. For another, he had sufficiently freed himself for the larger public ministry for which he was thereafter noted. In addition to the ecumenical and social organizations already cited, he was active in the Democratic Party and the AFL-CIO. In the latter he was the only minister regularly participating and he was eventually awarded its chaplaincy. He attached himself to the American Friends Service Committee, claiming that he found compatibility with these Quakers and others devoted to peace and world need. He also joined the Fellowship of Reconciliation and the War Resisters League. Therefore, when he startled North Carolina and the South in 1965 with his telegram to President Johnson condemning the Vietnam war, he was out of character not in the least.

Once again Finlator was accepting new challenges. His devotion to civil liberties became for him almost a second vocation. By the 1970s he was on the national board of both the ACLU and Southerners for Economic Justice and had begun his ten-year chairmanship of the North Carolina Advisory Committee to the U. S. Civil Rights Commission. His literary output, in the early years restricted principally to denominational house organs, now reached a wider audience. One national magazine, *Churchman*, published twenty-two of his articles between 1967 and 1983.

Finlator's political theology was mostly formulated piecemeal and on the run without time for rigorous research or formal construction. It tended to emerge as a reaction to crises, which in Finlator's case seem to appear in rapid succession. Nonetheless, early in his ministry, he had formulated a major position paper quite decisive for his later career, and published it as "The Prophetic Ministry" in 1952. As he defined a "prophetic ministry,"

In compassion God speaks to the human community through certain rare, called persons. Those who authentically represent God interpret the activity of God in social history. They answer the presence of God in the midst of political and economic life; they foretell the judgment and hope that are implicit in the loyalties and practices of the common life; and they set forth the vision of covenantal renewal. . . . The ministry must be all of this; otherwise it can really be a sort of cop-out and a desire to escape from the awesome and shaking prophetic word.[3]

This proclamation marked a turning point in Finlator's career, as he himself has recently noted.

Hitherto, even with college and seminary degrees, I had lived in a state of innocence, and I observed that the majority of my fellow ministers were content to live and move and have their being in the same innocence, and that from our Baptist seminaries there issued forth each year hundreds of the same! Not an exciting prospect. . . . It is the high task of the minister to make the congregation aware of low wages, ill housing, deficient nutrition, medical indigence, and economic injustice and how these things came to be. The minister's concern, if it is seen to be biblically based and as a part of total Christian commitment, can be infectious and compelling, but it will not happen in the congregation unless it happens in the ministry.[4]

The state of innocence Finlator mentioned pertains to the "academic" nature of his formal education. The outstanding professors of his college and seminary had provided him with solid classical learning, but when he faced the "real world" he felt cheated.

They taught me the classical languages, Latin and Greek, and the literary masterpieces, and how to use a library. Were they alive today they would, for the most part, disavow responsibility for some of the things that I have said and done, but I would lovingly remind them that their own largeness of heart and aca-

---

[3]Finlator, "The Prophetic Ministry," *Crozer Seminary Quarterly* 29 (Winter 1952): 39.

[4]Finlator, "The Ministry and Economic Justice," *Review & Expositor* 81 (Spring 1984): 246.

demic integrity will not let them off the hook so easily. . . . If professors keep opening minds, well, there is a risk. . . . Still I must admit the hardest part of growing up is to see the true size of one's mentors, and to go beyond them.[5]

What influenced Finlator most was the wider reading he was doing during the years of his early pastorates, when he in turn was producing a column nearly every week for several years in the *Biblical Recorder*. He read magazines such as the *Christian Century* and *Christianity and Crisis* and immersed himself in Reinhold Niebuhr. Niebuhr and Karl Barth and Dietrich Bonhoeffer were his new mentors, setting the agenda for his dealings with the world. Barth stipulated "that the Church must concentrate first on the lowest levels of human society. The poor, and the socially and economically weak and threatened, will always be the object of its primary and particular concern." Bonhoeffer wrote from within prison walls that "God Almighty sees the events of world history from below, from the perspective of the outcast, the suspects, the maltreated, the powerless, the oppressed, the reviled—in short from the perspective of those who suffer."

These words echo again and again when Finlator comes to formulating his own political theology.

> The more I understand Christian faith, the more I see the Bible is concerned with justice. And I've found that if God has any prejudice at all, He's prejudiced on the side of the poor and deprived and underprivileged.[6]
>
> The Scriptures tell us that the Messiah who was to come and the Messiah who did come, and is ever coming, identifies His mission and His message with the underprivileged, the powerless, the alienated, the blind and the lame and the suppressed. If the church ever realizes that God is on the side of these people and is summoning us to their cause, all of these fabricated axioms and myths about welfare people will be clobbered, every mountain of pride and self illusion will be brought low; every valley or rut shall be filled, and we shall make straight in the

---

[5]Ibid., 247.
[6]Quoted in *Raleigh* (NC) *Times,* 6 September 1965, 6.

desert highways for our God. And when we have ministered unto the least of God's children we have done unto Him.[7]

Requested by the Baptist association of Henderson, North Carolina, to speak to that strike-torn town in 1959, Finlator gave a major exposition of his political theology, published in the Raleigh *News and Observer*.

> To win the victory means we must give to the pulpit, or should I say *restore* to the pulpit, that freedom in responsibility through which alone the gospel can be proclaimed in its fullness and without fear. Laymen must learn to hear the hard sayings of the gospel, and, though in disagreement, support their ministers in their right and obligation to say them. Nothing can be so disastrous to the integrity of preaching as the economic insecurity of the minister. . . . Only as we clean house, only as we let the church be the church, can we speak the word of healing and reconciliation to the world. Only as our churches cease to be private clubs and become the houses of prayer for all peoples can we say to others, "Go and do likewise." Only as churches become again what the Supreme Court has been called, the conscience of the nation, can we say to the world, "This is the way: walk ye in it."[8]

Needless to say, Finlator's own attempt to embody this conception of the ministry tended to isolate him within his denominational structure. Cut off from any appointments to positions of responsibility or to ecclesiastical platforms, he resorted to writing letters of constructive criticism to the denominational journals and to presenting resolutions on specific social concerns to denominational conventions at the state and national level. For more than forty years he pestered nearly every official gathering of Southern Baptists with resolutions from the floor, in the time period designated by parliamentary proceedings for such resolutions and other unannounced business. Probably no other delegate offered so many resolutions about so many subjects. Other delegates must have thought that he had an inexhaustible supply. Sometimes the radical nature of the subject matter he pre-

---

[7]Finlator, speech in Toledo OH, 6 December 1979.
[8]Finlator, "Four Areas of Concern," *Biblical Recorder* 125 (7 November 1959): 12-13.

sented caught this middle-of-the-road body off guard. Sometimes he flooded a single session with multiple resolutions, apparently thinking that "saturation bombing" might occasionally hit the target. Parliamentary strategy might delay his efforts and might tone down the language of his resolutions, but no matter how much they managed to deter him, Baptist leaders could count on two things: Finlator would be back on the floor and he would speak to them in a courtly and forgiving manner. They, on their part, were not always so generous or so rule-abiding.

"My sole purpose is to put an issue before Baptists, knowing it will get nowhere. . .a matter of quietly educating my Baptist brethren," is the way Finlator described his strategy in 1973.[9] Whether he accomplished much change of heart among Baptists is questionable. However, over the years many persons expressed appreciation for his work. In a letter of 25 May 1982, a Virginia pastor wrote,

> When I attended my first North Carolina Baptist State Convention, I asked someone who that nut was that offered *that* resolution. That was 12 or 14 years ago, and it was only about the time that I moved from North Carolina to Virginia that I began to appreciate the fact that you were the pricker of conscience among us Baptists. . . . You never let us get too comfortable about a lot of things. You were a prophet in our midst—a pricker of our conscience.

A more unpromising tool for social change could hardly be found, and many believed it was totally ineffectual. Dr. Mark Corts, president of the North Carolina Convention in 1980, actually advised that the practice of submitting resolutions should be ended. Marshall Frady had earlier ridiculed the practice.

> It has managed, in the past, to provide a certain amount of eloquent floundering at general convention sessions, with some sporting resolutions about justice and brotherhood, that vaguely resembled conscience-wrestling. But since their convention resolutions amount to no more than simple expressions of opinion, binding no congregation, those flounderings have been aca-

---

[9]Quoted in *Winston-Salem* (NC) *Journal*, 28 May 1973, 11.

demic, and they usually end in a kind of compounded impotence, with the rejection of the resolution anyway.[10]

Obviously Finlator did not share this cynical appraisal. For him those resolutions had an educational value, informing an unconcerned public and appealing to the moral passion latent in every person. Finlator was convinced that they worked liked Gandhi's "truth-force" or what the Quakers call "truth to power." Finlator never spelled out his philosophy on the point, but in a strongly worded letter dispatched to all Baptist journals on 6 May 1970 he emphasized the principle. Dr. Lee Porter, first vice-president of the Southern Baptist Convention, had suggested that the parliamentary procedure requiring the resolution to be read aloud during the sessions should no longer be the accepted practice. Finlator protested his ruling.

> But all this is nonetheless a departure and a loss. We lose the drama of a messenger confronting his thousands of fellow messengers with a matter that has long lain on his heart. We lose the force of his rhetoric, the resonance of his convictions, the flash of his eye, the pulse of his feelings. We lose the opportunity to learn from his own words by what reasoning and persuasion he was led to formulate his resolution and how it squares with our Baptist faith and principles. And we also lose that throb of sympathy or surge of opposition which we experience in a free and open confrontation.

The traits spelled out so carefully here finally won for Finlator a great triumph at the 1981 Southern Baptist Convention in Los Angeles, his last official appearance before that massive deliberative body. He even raised a couple of laughs. The presiding officer interrupted him to question the necessity of reading the whole resolution. Finlator, maintaining his composure, protested audibly, "The interruptions, Mr. President, have destroyed the effectiveness of my *whereases!*" and went right on dramatically reading his statement. His resolution sought to expose the tactics of the Religious Right, of which many of the delegates were members. The resolution concluded:

---

[10]Frady, "God and Man," 40.

That the Southern Baptist Convention . . . deplore and reject the arrogation of the right of any group to define and pronounce for all people what is the Christian faith, and to seek through political means to impose this faith upon the American people under a government which is mandated to safeguard and respect the people of all religions and no religion.

The resolution passed, garnering headlines in major dailies from Florida to Detroit, and was the single action of the Convention to capture national news coverage.

For thirty-five years Finlator had had plenty of practice in introducing resolutions, though not with the same success. In a 1946 editorial he had contended:

Christian Frontiers is not unaware of the risks denominational unanimity and harmony will run if such resolutions are brought before the Convention, but it feels strongly that the time to run those risks has come. . . . This is the time for Southern Baptists to lift up their voices with strength and without fear, to speak the prophetic word and pronounce the divine judgement on issues so clearly and unavoidably freighted with Christian significance.[11]

He became the main practitioner of what he advocated. His resolutions were nearly always controversial: pressing Baptist colleges to abandon racism (1958), supporting ecumenicity by endorsing the New Delhi meeting of the World Council of Churches (1961), calling for the Negro Baptists to combine the two conventions in one meeting (1964), banning capital punishment (1964), favoring the sale of alcoholic beverages in public eating places (1966), approving reparations in response to the Black Manifesto (1970), opposing censorship of church publications (1971), pleading for public schools versus the Christian academies (1972), censuring President Gerald Ford's pardon of Richard Nixon (1974), advocating the decriminalization of marijuana (1977), approving the abolition of tax exemption of church properties (1978). These are but a few of the resolutions he brought

---

[11]Finlator, "More Resolutions Please," *Christian Frontiers* 1 (May 1946): 140.

before the convention year after year. One may imagine the reception they received.

Finlator's worst reception came at the State Convention in Asheville in 1967 when he first tried to submit his resolution against the Vietnam war. The press reported that he "was hissed and booed, with some shouting from the floor, 'Send Finlator to Vietnam!'" The presiding officer treated his motion with noticeable contempt and cooperated in an abuse of parliamentary procedure that prevented it from ever reaching the Resolutions Committee for consideration, much less to be voted on by the assembly. Finlator himself, in a letter to Frank Porter Graham soon afterwards, reported that "I never saw such an instant hissing en masse to reject with vigorous determination those resolutions which I had presented and to which I was so deeply attached." On 17 November he had written to William Gramley, a Moravian clergyman who had early opposed the war and consequently lost his pastorate because of his protest, "Have you ever been picketed, and especially at a church convention? Well, it is exciting, to say the least." Beyond the convention hall Finlator was ridiculed by Jesse Helms in his commentary for WRAL-TV, 17 November 1967.

> The most encouraging report of the Baptist State Convention's rejection of Rev. W. W. Finlator's proposed resolution on Vietnam is not that the Baptists rejected it, but that they rejected it with such swiftness that no doubt remains as to the question of Rev. Finlator's lack of influence within his own denomination. Hereafter, no matter how much publicity the gentleman receives from the "liberal press," he has now overplayed his hand. . . . Ironically it was the Rev. Finlator's insatiable appetite for publicity that did him in.

Earlier that year, functioning as a member of the Public Affairs Committee, Finlator had insisted in a letter to the committee, dated 10 April, "that Baptists protect one another within the fellowship of dissent." After the fracas at the Convention he penned a lengthy appeal for proper parliamentary procedure.

> I was under no illusions—I dared not ever hope—regarding a favorable report from the Resolutions Committee of my an-

nounced proposals. The best I could expect, and had the right to expect, was honest confrontation and debate first by the committee and later by the Convention in session. This procedure would have been in accordance with our Baptist tradition and practice. But when the Convention, which has always prided itself as a free and open deliberative Baptist body, immediately invoked cloture, refused to allow the proposals to be referred to the Resolutions Committee, and thereby precluded any possibility of confrontation with what is universally considered the greatest issue of our day, I was shocked and am deeply disturbed. For this I was totally unprepared and, honestly, my concern now is for something more than the fate of those proposals. . . . It is for ourselves.

Yet, forgive me, for I truly harbor no messianic feelings at all, when I presented these proposals the response seemed to be, "Away with this man! For we will hear nothing from him." But to the fiasco was added self delusion—on the part of the Convention. Immediately after cloture had been voted the President was ready with instructions to the news media that they clearly understand this vote to mean that North Carolina Baptists had taken no action on the Vietnam proposal at all. To the world he was saying that while washing our hands of the whole matter we had taken no action! But alas, the decision to do nothing is still decision—and commitment. We have not thereby absolved ourselves, and we do grievously err if we allow the President, or our conscience, to lay that flattering unction to our souls.[12]

Many delegates felt as Finlator did about his shabby treatment, and they wrote to him expressing their dismay and encouragement. The many letters originated from all levels of Baptists. One minister wrote,

Just a word to say that I share your disappointment in the handling of your resolution—it would have been such a step forward for the Convention. I still believe, however, that by speaking year after year you are chipping away a little apathy, causing some to think, and gaining a few in the vote. At least no one can say that there hasn't been a witness—and that is important, even

---

[12]Finlator, "Letter to the Editor," *Charity and Children* 81 (30 November 1967): 2.

if it only becomes important in the years ahead when the spirit of your motion is generally held and the history books report that you were right but too early (in actuality you are right, early and yet "smack-dab" in the middle of God's right time and right place.) Keep going at it!

An employee in the Baptist state headquarters wrote,

> Just a note to let you know how much I appreciate you. Don't give up on us. We need the constant prodding of your thinking and convictions. Perhaps one of these days we will "graduate" to your level of justice and concern.

An associate minister wrote,

> I too appreciated what you are doing to keep before us as Baptists the weightier matters of the Law—war, race, poverty. I liked both of the resolutions. . . . I sometimes feel if it weren't for you, we'd seldom discuss anything significant in our conventions.

And another preacher added,

> I would like to take this opportunity to let you know of my appreciation for the courageous Christian stands that you have taken before the Baptists of North Carolina down through the years. I agree with John Lewis that our convention should be extremely grateful for "Socratic flies like Bill Finlator who keep our state attention focused upon decisive Christian issues." I have been in the ministry for the last nine years, and I have observed you many times as you took unpopular, though thoroughly Christian, positions on questions before our Convention. . . . It is encouraging indeed to those of us younger ministers who believe in the *total* Gospel for the *total* man to find a man of your stature and calibre in our denomination.

Naturally the intensity of opposing views about the Vietnam war colored the reception of Finlator's resolutions as he offered them year after year. Yet at that moment of history, Southern Baptists were among the few major American denominations that had not censured the war. The superpatriotic Southland, with its militaristic tradition and loyalty to a Democratic administration, provided few forums for Finlator's analysis. Referring to his reception at the Methodist College situated near Ft. Bragg, Finlator revealed in a letter of 1969 that "I just escaped being lynched!" Wingate College closed its doors to him. A Raleigh PTA canceled his speech. Thus the Baptist Convention can hardly be viewed as extraordinarily blameworthy for its lack of action during this time.

It was Finlator's high opinion of the unique Baptist appreciation of dissent that gave him cause to grieve over how the Convention treated his many resolutions. In 1963, he had argued that healthy controversy over critical social issues "far from threatening us [should] mean that Baptists have been shaken to their own first principles. In the name of our history and witness we should lead the way and welcome the change." For Finlator the genius of Baptists resides in their radical dissent against a religion that cheapens itself into a civic faith. He often bragged that "we are a denomination born in dissent, conceived among a persecuted minority." It was precisely this element within the Baptist tradition that had produced the few prophets like himself. In response to a letter attacking him and others for standing on the streets in silent vigil against the Vietnam war, labeling them "a laughable lot," he wrote on 3 May 1967, "Dissent is never easy, particularly in critical times such as are these days. But we feel that it is all the more necessary to give expression of dissent at such a time."

The one occasion he was privileged to serve on the North Carolina Baptist Public Affairs Committee came during the 1960s when white preachers supporting the civil rights movement jeopardized their pulpits and the few voices opposing the Vietnam war were being suppressed. Finlator penned the section of the report adopted at the Asheville Convention of 1967.

> The majority opinion of any given society is often not the right opinion. Wise people look for truth and reality as they float to the surface in the boiling seas of social unrest. The less wise can think of nothing but the stifling of protest and the killing off of dissent. The society which does this blinds itself to possible deficiencies. True, the demonstration of protest and dissent is frequently an ugly episode. It heats up the passions of all concerned until the lava of violence may pour over the slopes in a destroying hate. Still protest and dissent offer striking opportunities for a cul-

ture, armed with its own mores and entrenched in its own customs, to see itself as it really is, to become self defensive of innovation, and to alter itself for the better.

"To paraphrase our Lord," Finlator often remarked, "I think there is more weeping in heaven over one dissenter squelched than over ninety-nine antidissident conservatives safely in the fold." One tactic in his overall strategy was periodically to introduce resolutions glorifying this side of the historic Baptist tradition. He could count on some routine allegiance to noble sounding words, just as Americans not in the least aware of the radical nature of the Bill of Rights may give lip service to it. After one of his resolutions passed without one negative vote at the 1978 North Carolina Baptist Convention meeting in Charlotte, Finlator wrote:

> My file contains letters mailed to me over the years from many fellow ministers supporting, in silence, views I have expressed and positions I have taken, but also from lay persons wishing their own ministers would say, and their own churches would act on, these same things. Knowing of the existence, shall I say, of these substantive Baptists, people more interested in depth than growth, more concerned for quality than quantity, more oriented to issues than to statistics, I introduced my resolution on the cherished Baptist principles.

Finlator took the matter of introducing resolutions seriously, but that was not always the case for his opponents. They tended to play down the effect of passing resolutions. Resolution time for many delegates was little more than a lark interspersed between the inspirational sermons and the necessary committee reports. For some the custom seemed an exercise in futility, for others an attention-getter, for others a necessary nuisance of democratic procedure. Dr. Mark Corts, a former president of the Convention, wrote in his church newsletter of 18 November 1981 "that resolutions mean nothing, and if they are not to be taken seriously, I question their value in the convention. . . . They are often the expression of concern of only a small number of messengers." Jesse Helms, the TV commentator later to become a U. S. Senator, himself a loyal Baptist, rarely missed an opportunity to depreciate Finlator's interjections.

> Time and time again, he has cluttered various forums, including the Baptist State Convention with his surprising, sometimes disguised resolutions and proposals. And sometimes, sleepy, unthinking Baptists voted aye only to find themselves embarrassed later. (WRAL Viewpoint, 17 November 1967).

In the light of the checkered success of his resolutions, the crowning irony of Finlator's career occurred when the North Carolina Convention paused to recognize his lifetime contribution as a presenter of resolutions. It was his last convention as an instated pastor in 1981. As usual, Finlator had taken the microphone to present one of his catchall resolutions. This time the "whereas" maintained that they

> who are strong must bear the infirmities of the weak, that from those to whom much is given much will be required, that God in Christ Jesus has identified with the hungry, the sick, the shelterless, the alienated and the imprisoned; . . . be it therefore resolved that the churches in an hour of crisis and anxiety allocate a greater portion of their resources, and that the government give high priority of concern and resources to the problems of health, housing, hunger and hopes of the people that, in massiveness and urgency, are beyond the capacity of churches and private agencies.

The chairman of the Resolutions Committee, Gaylord Laymon, interrupted Finlator to read a resolution of appreciation.

> For many years this convention has heard the introductory identification, "My name is W. W. Finlator from Raleigh." A resolution would immediately follow. Over the years Bill Finlator has given the Resolutions Committee more work than any other person. Sometimes you voted for the resolution: sometimes you voted against it; sometimes you tabled it. But always that resolution was a pricking of our corporate conscience concerning a cherished freedom, or a call for greater concern for the poor, the oppressed, and the victimized in our society. Before this convention convenes next year, Bill Finlator will retire from the pastorate of Pullen Church. On behalf of our Committee I wish to

thank Bill Finlator for being a persistent voice for the application of the Christian Gospel to *all* of life.

Had Finlator pressed his luck as a gadfly? He was conscious of afflicting Baptists with his endless resolutions, egging them on, agitating them, reminding them of their self-professed heights, calling them back to their radical roots. He excused his persistence by insisting that

> while I seem always to be a part of His Majesty's Kingdom, I've always thought one has an obligation within the church to understand it, to appreciate it, to grow on it, to transcend it, yes. It took a lot of grace on the part of both sides in order for us to accept each other. But I do believe the church must lead the way. And I think that Baptists have gained a great deal of social awareness. While my "far out" resolutions may have been way ahead of them, the truth of the matter is that the Baptist Convention has come around to adopting in principle some of them. I never expected anything like immediate success and I was aware, even when I went down, I was scoring points, really registering an effect.

What Finlator did in prompting Baptists he also applied to the political leaders—executive, judicial, legislative and bureaucratic. His bailiwick was the North Carolina Legislature and, to a more limited extent, the U. S. Congress. As chairman of the legislative committee for the North Carolina Civil Liberties Union (the CLU had held its organizational meeting in the Pullen church) for more than twenty years and for a short time chairman of the same committee for the North Carolina Council of Churches, he was constantly around when the state assembly was in session. Finlator gave himself the task of reminding his fellow citizens of their pretensions to democracy in the same manner in which he challenged Baptists to practice the teachings of the New Testament. For Finlator the location of his pulpit in the governing center of the state was an advantage. Once the downtown Sir Walter Hotel closed, what was called "the second legislature" moved west on Hillsborough Street to the deluxe motels next to Pullen. And Finlator certainly had no qualms about mixing politics and religion. His self-appointed role as watchdog of the legislature quickly earned him the title "political parson."

However, long before his Raleigh residency, Finlator had become known for his political "meddling." He came to state attention in 1950 in leading Currituck County to rid itself of legalized gambling. Subsequently, he took on such issues as the inequities in the state law schools provided for whites and blacks (1950), anticommunism of the McCarthy brand (1952), censorship (1953), and Governor Luther Hodges's resistance to desegregation (1954). Within his first four years of coming to Pullen, he had had a speech inserted for the first time in the *Congressional Record* (by Senator Lyndon Johnson in 1957) and his first appointment as a United Nations Associate (under Frank Graham's guidance in 1958); he had intervened in the trial of the labor leader Boyd Payton (1959) and had opposed Beverly Lake's candidacy for governor on grounds of racism (1960).

Finlator was never elected to any political office, either in the church or state, but he appreciated the role of the ordinary citizen within the democratic process. Wherever there was a governmental hearing for citizen initiatives, one could count on Finlator's presence. He constantly harangued political leaders with his public letters. No fat-salaried lobbyist has likely matched his persistence and presence during the twenty years from 1960 to 1980. Finlator seems to have conceived of himself as the poor man's lobbyist. He apparently relished keeping the legislature on its toes, for the record of his appearances before its committee hearings is extensive.

His critics were quick to question his ability to walk the line separating church and state with equanimity. Finlator replied that

> I never felt that I was too political. No one knows me well could ever have suspected me of wanting political power. I have never wanted to be a politician and have always hoped I could remain a minister. I did feel that the church is as good a place to achieve or to help achieve desired political change, or changes which are brought about by political leadership. I have never wanted to do anything political that would advance the church I serve or the denomination I belong to or religion in general. So I am not a "po-

litical parson," but I do believe with Aristotle that every person
is a political animal.

With that rationale, Finlator tirelessly addressed the political issues of his day. While he managed not to force religion on
the state, some people felt that he did a considerable amount of
"forcing" politics on his own congregation. Sermon topics repeatedly emphasized mixing politics and religion, and often single
sermons were devoted to a specific political issue. Usually, when
the legislature opened its new year, he devoted a sermon to the
bills needed; at the conclusion of its sessions, he had a sermon
evaluating its accomplishments. Many of these sermons were reported by the state and national press.

Finlator's concern about the deprivation of rights generally
gained the most attention. Over the years newspaper headlines
emphasized his prophetic candor: "What's Right, What's Wrong
in North Carolina" (27 March 1960); "North Carolina First in
Repression" (26 October 1975); "North Carolina Branded No. 1 in
Suppression" (4 September 1976); "Finlator Says North Carolina
Deserves Nasty Image" (18 December 1980). Newspaper headlines also tended to present a negative view of his endeavors. One
might get the impression that Finlator was less than loyal to his
state and nation. On the contrary, he professed to love them with
a prophetic zeal, as is typified in one of the speeches cited. Playing on the slogan, "First in Freedom," which had just been im-
printed on every automobile license plate in the state, Finlator
wondered how

> North Carolina, which for many years enjoyed the reputation of
> the most open, most progressive, most freedom-loving state in the
> South, has now, in our day, become in the eyes of the world the
> most regressive state in the union. . . . Whatever happened to
> North Carolina that she should fall from grace so precipitately?

He then listed the dismal facts to support his contention about the
demise of freedom: only North Carolina among all states retains
the outlaw statute; industrial unionism is lowest in North Carolina; persons such as the Wilmington Ten languish in prison with
unconscionably long and punitive sentences; the state has the

highest percentage of its people behind bars and the largest number on death row.[13] In another public statement he reminded his audience that his catalogue was not new to their ears.

> Our own church bodies have condemned the practice of capital punishment and decried the plight of migrant laborers; our local citizens' groups have exposed the harsh sentences and the inhuman conditions of our prison system; our bar associations and our civil liberties groups have questioned the outlaw statute and other discriminatory laws still on the books; our labor leaders have cried out against the anti-unionism and right-to-work laws that have kept North Carolina on the very bottom of the industrial wages and incomes; the N.C. Advisory Committee on Civil Rights has documented the economic and political deprivation of Indian, black and other minority citizens and questioned whether the administration of justice has at times served as an instrument of justice and our perceptive newspaper editors and university scholars have written of the denial of full citizenship and opportunity throughout the State.[14]

As something of a dissident himself, Finlator was particularly sensitive to any signs of suppression of dissent in society. Writing to the civil rights lawyer Jerry Paul on 4 October 1973, he was apprehensive about

> whether there is a systematic use of courts and jails to suppress dissent. We charge communist countries for doing precisely this. We in turn must never use the structures of criminal justice to suppress dissent. And in religious circles we must never bury creative dissent under the cloak of supercilious piety and false unity.

In a statement to the Interreligion Task Force on Criminal Justice on 30 June 1978, he pursued the seriousness of his charge.

> I hope that the task force, in addition to the areas of concern you have already embraced, will take a hard look at the issue of suppression of dissent from coast to coast by the criminal justice system. Now this is something you just don't go around mention-

---

[13]"First in Repression," *Asheville* (NC) *Citizen* 4 September 1976, 4.
[14]Quoted in *News and Observer* (Raleigh NC), 6 September 1976, 14.

ing in polite society. The charge that the instruments of law and justice in America could ever be used to stifle free speech and action or to suppress minorities is totally unacceptable. . . . But you are meeting in North Carolina where some celebrated cases argue eloquently to the contrary. There is the famous Gastonia strike a couple of generations back; there is the communist trial of Junius Scales in Chapel Hill; there is the crackdown and imprisonment of Boyd Payton and other textile worker-leaders in Henderson just a few years ago; and currently there is the Charlotte Three and there is the Wilmington Ten. The awful spectre of political prisoners hangs heavy on North Carolina jurisprudence. . . . Your draft statement quite appropriately refers to capital punishment. It says nothing, as I recall, about the use of capital punishment, particularly in the southeast, as a means of intimidating and controlling a segment of our population. . . . In short nothing can be so destructive of our total system of jurisprudence, and so destructive of faith in the rule of law and respect for the courts than the perversion of the criminal system into a means of suppression of dissent.

Loyalty and love did not mean for Finlator reluctance to criticize. To the contrary, one's love is measured by the extent and depth of the criticism one brings to enrich the beloved. Finlator loved his Israel like the prophets of old. With a patriot's fervor he often began his criticism with lines taken from the unofficial state anthem.

> Here's to the land of the longleaf pine,
> The summer land where the sun doth
> shine,
> Where the weak grow strong and the
> strong grow great,
> Here's to "down home," the old North
> State!

However, as he read the signs of the times, it was "surely in such a climate most difficult for the weak to grow strong and the strong to grow great." Always identifying himself as a native Southerner who had never lived outside the South, he reveled in its culture. He celebrated it in an article entitled "A Southerner's Good Life," widely reproduced, but first printed in the *Charlotte Ob-*

server, 3 May 1977. Similarly, he always identified himself as a *Southern* Baptist *preacher.* Being Southern and Christian meant for Finlator that "political duty is religious."

> Politics is not a dirty but a beautiful word; so let's be unblush-ingly political, all of us . . . I can hear people saying: This is a preacher writing about politics and government and he has hardly mentioned God, the Bible and the Church. Why doesn't he stop his meddling and stick to preaching the gospel? Well, the gospel has something to say about all this too. Listen to Jesus of Naza-reth: "For I was hungry and ye gave me meat; I was thirsty and ye gave me drink; I was a stranger and ye took me in; naked and ye clothed me; I was sick and ye visited me; I was in prison, and ye came to me." . . . If anyone knows a non-political way of deal-ing with massive hunger, massive sickness, massive poor hous-ing, massive prison reform, and doing it realistically, I should love to hear from him. In my judgment you can't be a Christian un-politically today.[15]

Finlator's critics upbraided him for violating his own cher-ished principle of separation of church and state. Such criticism came from those who felt his "bleeding heart" might interfere with their vested interests and from some Christians who felt his mes-sage had become altogether the gospel of civil liberties. Typical of the latter is a letter from an old friend, a pastor in Fayetteville, written on 25 February 1981.

> Do you really believe in legalizing prostitution, homosexu-ality and marijuana? Or has your chairmanship of the legisla-tive committee of N.C.C.L.U. forced you into propagandizing something in which you do not personally believe? I have always thought of you as a prophet willing to risk your reputation for the underdog. I'm going on loving you as a friend, but I do hope you have not confused personal permissiveness with social justice. If the water gets too hot, keep in mind that you may be adding fuel to the fire under your pot.

---

[15]Finlator, "Political Duty Is Religious," *Charlotte* (NC) *Observer,* 18 Janu-ary 1970, A1.

Typical of another kind of criticism is a letter from Chub Sewell, published 1 May 1963 in the Raleigh *News and Observer*. Sewell was a lawyer who had gained something of a reputation for his rhetoric in that paper over the years.

> Integration is part of the social gospel. The social gospel is the satanic substitute for the true gospel of grace. The Social Gospel tries to bring in the kingdom of God but denies the king. Social gospel do-gooders, up-lifters, reformers and kingdom of God fetchers, like the Rev. Mr. Finlator, are not interested in a Person but in a high-class program. They are now on a program to re-write the Bible, neutralize sin, galvanize humanity, air-condition hell and make the world such a beautiful, quiet and peaceful place that the Lord will look down from heaven with some degree of astonishment and decide to move in with us in order to be more comfortable.

Politicians whose prominence demands response to all their correspondence tended to give Finlator an extra nod. While they certainly did not always agree with his promotion of certain causes, they tended to respect Finlator's efforts to influence them. Congressman Ike Andrews wrote on 1 June 1982:

> Your obvious dedication, social consciousness and unlimited energy have propelled you to a position in our country which commends our admiration and respect. For as long as the need for social change and improvement exists, I know we will be hearing from you.

It was not always easy for Finlator to function in two roles, as preacher and as promoter of civil liberties. On one occasion, as chairman of the ACLU legislative committee, he proposed "to decriminalize offenses that are generally considered victimless and that are largely in the area of alcoholic consumption, drugs, and intimacy." One newspaper twisted this into "the decriminalization of consentual activities—such as sexual practices between consenting adults committed in private, including heterosexual and homosexual acts and prostitution." He addressed this dilemma in an appearance before the North Carolina Senate Judiciary Subcommittee on 29 March 1977.

It is not an enviable role for a clergyman, and a Southern Baptist at that, to take a public stand in opposition to proposed legislation the intent of which is the control of pornography. It is only that I fear obscenity less than censorship that I ask you to defeat Senate Bill 165, and any subsequent legislation that would give the government power to bypass procedures and safeguards built into our judicial system to protect freedom. I understand the strong feeling of my fellow ministers and others who have appeared before you last week and I have no propensity to advocacy for the purveyors of pornography . . . but there are times when a preacher, like a politician, must hold his nose and vote and that is the manner in which I cast my ballot today against Senate Bill 165.

Another example of the seeming conflict of interests accompanying his political participation was his defense of the constitutional rights of the hate groups such as the Ku Klux Klan, the John Birch Society and the American Nazi Party. No matter how much he personally and as a Christian might despise these groups—knowing what they stand for, how they victimize people, undermine democracy, and blaspheme the Christian religion—Finlator nonetheless found himself in the awkward position of defending their civil rights. Again, before a legislative committee on 8 April 1968, he presented his reasons.

We will defend a Klansman not because he belongs to the Ku Klux Klan, a member of the John Birch Society not because of his strongly held views, a socialist not because of his socialism, but because it has been determined in either case that his rights as a citizen have been infringed. Our interest in legislation reflects, and reflects solely this same concern for the basic liberties of each person as a citizen.

In this instance, the KKK "rewarded" Finlator's labors in its behalf by making him the target of its wrath in the telephone recording service it sponsored!

In response to his detractors, who held that he was less a minister of the gospel than a minister of the law, preaching more from the Bill of Rights than from the Bible, he vigorously contended that he treated them as twins, inextricably bound together. "You must remember, my Baptist tradition holds to the literalness of the Sermon and contributed by suffering whiplashes to the particulars of the Bill." He saw no conflict. He suspected the real danger was from those Christians "who side with the lowest level of the law and wrap that position up in the gospel." "What we desperately need," he argued, "is the gospel speaking to the law. I would like to think that I have spent my time doing the latter, pursuing the spiritual radicalness implicit in the basic American documents." For him the principle of separation of church and state never implies that church people and churches themselves not participate in politics.

> When the church withdraws from the political life of society to protect its purity it ends by becoming the very thing it sought to escape. For when the church has said to politics, You render to Caesar and we shall render to God, the church has already become a replica of the society it adjures. And society will never be transformed or redeemed by a replica of itself.

Finlator's political theology was anything but a replica of the South. Instead it sought to transcend the cultural mythos and "to redeem the times" by a vigorous and creative application of the radical aspects of the Bible, the Baptist heritage, and the Bill of Rights.

Chapter Two

ENJOYING CONTROVERSY

"WHEN I WAS A YOUNG LAD growing up in eastern North Carolina, I went to revival meetings which often found the preacher praising God and damning a certain Bill Finlator." This account reflects the early years of Finlator's controversial career. By 1982, the year of his retirement, a newspaper man, the youngest of three generations who had watched and secretly admired Finlator's public posture, summed up that career. Writing in the *Greensboro Daily News,* Jim Jenkins declared,

> Many have disagreed with his social and political views. Many have thought he went too far on occasion. But whether he has been standing in front of the altar performing a wedding or with his head bowed leading a peace vigil, there has never been any doubt that the stance was firm. The wisdom of his convictions has been fired upon many times, but the courage behind them is unscarred. And courage can get you into trouble. Finlator has known

this for a long time, but it has never kept him from taking the path that was covered in brush and thorns.[1]

Those impressions, separated by some thirty years, convey something of Finlator's reputation as a person of controversy.

During the decades that span these two impressions Finlator was indeed engaged in many heated debates, debates that he gave every indication of enjoying. Asked once why he was involved in so many controversies, he laughed the question aside.

> Controversy is exciting, and I like exciting things. Put another way, a minister has to be three things: bold, brassy and something of a ham. At times I have been all three. As a matter of fact, the pulpit is always in the limelight and to occupy the pulpit Sunday after Sunday without making a difference, without really stirring the people, without agitating for the Lord, may be a big sin.

Even in retirement he still advised having fun. Requested by the social studies teachers of North Carolina to expound on how to handle hot issues, Finlator expressed his philosophy as reported in the *Charlotte News.* "People who are willing to take a stand have more fun," Finlator said. "They don't need drugs to stimulate them. Their whole lives are full of adrenaline. When you get involved in these things, your life is full of joy and excitement. You can't afford to die." He argued that the cost of not taking a stand is too high. "The heart of it is, you have to take a stand, because if you don't others will. My not taking a stand gives them the green light. Not to take a stand is to commit what Martin Luther called 'wicked silence.' "

There is no doubt that Finlator was enamored by the limelight all this controversy brought him. His wife recalls the time when a newsman and his spouse came to their home seeking shelter from the public abuse resulting from his published endorsement of the civil rights demonstrations. The man's wife, an-

---

[1] Jim Jenkins, "The Untold Story of Bill Finlator," *Greensboro* (NC) *Daily News,* 23 May 1982, F1.

[2] Quoted in "Sermons to Teachers," *Charlotte* (NC) *News,* 25 February 1983, 5.

gered by the hate mail and phone calls, turned to Mary Lib Finlator and inquired, somewhat desperately, whether she had similar feelings when her husband was under attack. "Yes," she replied with aplomb, "I did until the day I began to suspect that Bill was actually enjoying it all."

Finlator's critics were quick to leap on this weakness. One North Carolina editor ridiculed him as a publicity seeker.

> Rev. Finlator has been called "controversial" mainly because he appears to take the opposite line of reasoning from every other freedom-loving American. We would not like to really think so but it appears to us that the Rev. Finlator does all this sometimes, perhaps all the time, to get the publicity for himself and his church in Raleigh he certainly would not get otherwise.[3]

Indeed, Finlator may be accused of cultivating this image. He certainly seems to have gained some satisfaction from the unexpected outcome of certain controversies. One such case was the cancellation of his speaking engagement at the Carrol Junior High School in Raleigh in 1969. As the *Raleigh Times* reported the incident, Richard Smith, the local PTA president responsible for blocking him said, "We didn't want Mr. Finlator or any other highly controversial figure to get up there and have the program to himself. Since this man is so highly controversial, we decided to cancel the program."[4] Overnight Finlator's telephone began ringing and letters came pouring in. His friends wanted to know how they could get themselves into the enviable predicament of not having to create Mickey Mouse homilies for PTA meetings. Finlator's amusement at the outcome is manifest in his response to one such inquiry.

> At this particular season of the year I am going about saying to myself "He was despised and rejected and he opened not his mouth." One or two have called or written by way of consolation that I am still welcome at the "Harper Valley PTA" and now comes your note about being banned in Boston or burned in Mississippi or blackballed by the Raleigh PTA. . . . The whole thing

---

[3]Editorial, *Dunn* (NC) *Daily Record,* 6 May 1970, 4.
[4]News Item, *Raleigh* (NC) *Times,* 18 March 1969, 11.

is a comedy of errors. And, to be truthful, there is a little bit of John Birch influence on the deal and I hope that I am not too unchristian when I express the joy of seeing it backfire in that direction. It seems that a man named Christ Smith, a bona fide John Bircher, called in to another Smith who was that way inclined. The second Smith happened to be the president of the PTA and he proceeded to take things into his own hands and call off the meeting lock, stock and barrel. This included the business meeting too. They had folks riding up that night, even after the loud speaker announcement at school, thinking there would be a meeting. Now I believe there is quite a furor but just imagine this at dear old Carrol where my sister used to teach.

Part of Finlator's penchant for controversy may be due to his feisty personality and his healthy enjoyment of a good fight. But the greater part derived from his proclivity to side with the underdog, his willingness to champion unpopular causes and his readiness to associate with "questionable" characters, giving each person the benefit of the doubt. That bent, in turn, was reinforced by his conception of religion—how God operates in the world. He was moved by a basic human identity such as that shared by James Russell Lowell in his definition of freedom, "to wear the chains our brothers and sisters wear," or by Eugene V. Debs, who said, "While there is a lower class, I am in it; while there is a criminal element, I am of it; while there is a soul in prison, I am not free."

One thing is sure: for a Southern Baptist preacher Finlator has found himself in strange company and odd places. A stranger embodiment of the Baptist preacher role hardly exists: chaplain to labor unions, civil libertarian, a friend of prisoners and of left-wing agitators and some of America's prominent social radicals—among them Carl and Ann Braden, Willard Uphaus, Norman Thomas, James Dombrowski, the Berrigan brothers, and Martin Luther King, Jr. He is a defender of the poor, of disenfranchised blacks, Indians and women, of student rebels and draft protesters. Although avowedly a Baptist preacher foremost and always, he succeeded in embarrassing not only many Baptists but also many others who shared a traditional and narrowly circumscribed conception of how a preacher should act in and out of the pulpit.

Nonetheless Finlator's fulfillment of the suburban, middle-class pastoral role was fairly routine. On the surface, he was a circumspect Southern gentleman, a dabbler in sports, literature, politics and family lineage, the good husband and father, the friendly neighbor and the loyal civic leader. Underneath these trappings was the advocate of the marginal people, those who had no voice and leverage for social change. Without prejudging them, he was ready to entertain their petition for redress. Wherever people's rights, liberties and humanity were in jeopardy, whether communists or Ku Klux Klanspeople, Moonies or American Nazis, migrants or harassed females, Finlator tried to respond. He seemed to find contact with liberal causes and the victimized more enthralling than the conventional world he encountered on the surface. He came to the side of Junius Scales, accused of being a communist (1962); David Andrews, suspended from his job as chaplain for the Methodist students at the state college in Boone because he protested the Vietnam war (1962); of Russell Brantley, the novelist employed by Wake Forest University whose portrait of "Jonathan Beam" so offended conservative Baptists (1962); of the three leaders of the Baptist Student Union fired from their jobs (1954); of the professors at Louisville Seminary (1959) and at Campbell College (1974) questionably relieved of their professorships; of labor leaders under duress like Boyd Payton (1959) and Wilbur Hobby (1980); of Ben Chavis and the Wilmington Ten (1976); of the black poet T. J. Reddy (1977), in prison as a result of a shoddy trial; of Marie Hill, the black teenager scheduled to be executed (Finlator brought her a guitar on death row, 1977); of Dan and Margaret McSurley, hounded by a U. S. Senate investigating committee (1978). Reading this record, one might conclude that Finlator went out of his way to invite trouble. He certainly did not hide his preferences. When *The Baptist Program* addressed the question of extremism on the right and the left, Finlator wrote to its editor on 31 October 1969 "The two sides are not equally threatening. . . . Naturally I don't regard the left with the same ominous feelings that I do the right, but then I am a thoroughly biased man!" In addressing his congregation

at Pullen in his final sermon before retirement on 20 June 1982,
he confessed, "I have often been in the fray, not often enough for
my conscience, too often, perhaps, for some of you."

As the years mounted Finlator found himself more and more
on the firing line, no longer confined to the state and the South
but embroiled on the national level. In the first year of his retirement, Finlator debated on three national television shows, was
rebutted by Nat Hentoff in a *Village Voice* article and published
articles in two national magazines. He spoke on platforms as far
afield as Pittsburgh, Louisville, and New York. His topics covered quite a spectrum: creationism and science in the schools,
President Reagan's proclamation on the Year of the Bible, PCB
contamination, nuclear-free zones, nuclear disarmament, tuition
grants to private schools, ecology, women's rights, laws protect-
ing migrants, death penalty, FBI powers, the Good Friday service of the North Carolina Assembly, legalized lottery, the
Christmas show at the state planetarium, the tanks provided by
the Pentagon to local National Guard units, and the expulsion of
illegal-entry Salvadorans. He defended communist party members arrested in Raleigh, the World Council of Churches, and
continued funding for abortion. He appeared before the U. S. Senate Judiciary Committee, once again elaborating his understanding of the principle of separation of church and state.

Finlator's lifelong resolve was expressed in the last paragraph of a 1983 *Christian Century* article. "For this cause" he
wrote "I propose to be both militant civil libertarian and authentic Baptist, both advocate of religious faith and opponent of religious coercion—looking to the day of a free church in a free society
and knowing my friends from my adversaries, whomever."[5] Over
the years, the "whomevers" had been many. Just one respondent
to the *Century* article will suffice to exhibit the nature of many
such adversaries. Kenneth Bragg, director of missions for the
Rowan Baptist Association, wrote to Finlator on 5 April 1983.

---

[5]W. W. Finlator, "They're Trying to Make Us Baptists," *Christian Century*,
100 (6 April 1983): 303.

I have just read your article in the *Christian Century*. Frankly, it makes me sick at the stomach. Do we need to embrace the atheism of Madalyn Murray O'Hair, the ACLU, and the humanist-liberals, as Southern Baptists? They may believe in the absolute separation of church and state, but for very different reasons. They would use this precious Baptist doctrine to attack and destroy the true Christian faith.

It may be that the ACLU is the most dangerous organization in America in its fight against the church. Atheism will prevail in these United States, as in Russia, thanks to people who would worship and deify MAN rather than the true God. Whose side are you really on, Mr. Finlator?

Finlator's appearance on the Phil Donahue television program on 9 December 1982 brought the largest amount of such mail. On that program devoted to President Reagan's proclamation of the Year of the Bible, Finlator argued that "while I am glad our president is a man of prayer, of faith with a religious conviction and believes in the Bible, I do not think he can use his office in any way to promote that. And when he does, he is thoughtless, unfeeling, and discriminating because millions of Americans are not church members, millions are atheists, humanists and other than the Christian faith." Questioned in an interview in the *Winston-Salem Sentinel* about his television stand, Finlator added,

I am a Southern Baptist who strongly opposes this action by the president as a violation of church and state separation, and a man who is vice-president of the ACLU which upholds the First Amendment. The President did not swear his oath of office to uphold the Ten Commandments or the Sermon on the Mount, but he is sworn to uphold the Constitution. I have found that the more presidents appeal to religion as presidents, the less they are faithful in carrying out their oath to uphold the Constitution. The president and government are not here to promote religion but justice and what we are doing in this country today is substituting religion for justice. That bothers me. You can run to religion and get away from justice. The implications are that there is a strong movement to make us believe that this is a Christian na-

tion and this movement centers in the President. Ours is not supposed to be a Christian nation.[6]

Of the flood of letters he received in opposition to the position he
expounded on that show, this note is typical.

> I have seen you on the Donahue show. I think the reason the
> news media of this world gives you attention is because you are
> a novelty—a man who claims to be a reverend, a Christian, a
> minister, and yet you hold such unChristian views, such im-
> moral views, and such anti-American views.
>
> I think I heard someone say once that what Jerry Falwell is
> to the Moral Majority you are to the Civil Liberties Union, ex-
> cept on a smaller scale, of course.
>
> Yes, you are religious and you are of the world and you use
> your carnal mind. I believe that you are just a publicity hound
> (you are egotistically seeking your own thing), you love contro-
> versy and argument.

For more than forty years Finlator had become accustomed to
such violent language as he stepped forth to defend the victimized or to affirm what he interpreted as genuine democracy and
authentic Christian faith. However as he moved more and more
into social activism, dividing his time between the safety of the
pastorate and the hazards of the public arena, he was unavoidably trapped in coalitions with some strange bedfellows and obliged
to make hasty judgments not always solidly supported by fact and
philosophy. As much as he tried to explain himself, he was not
able to satisfy his critics. Moreover, he had not always been so "far
out." Few signs at the outset of his ministry provide any premo-
nition of what he was to become. He began his preaching career
in 1937 in Pittsboro and never departed those Eastern North
Carolina environs for fifty years, but he was transformed from a
typical pastor shepherding his sheep into a man at odds with his
times. Finlator admits that his stance was "fairly innocuous" in
the early days. "Still, from the first I came to know personally the
black preachers and the black principal and teachers and I spoke

---

[6]"Persistent Preacher Speaks Out," *Winston-Salem* (NC) *Sentinel,* 10 December 1982, 10.

in their churches and schools," he recalls. "I remember opposing our coming entry into World War II and stirring up the wrath of the local American Legion. And I did establish friendship with other submerged groups, such as labor. But still, I can think of nothing rash in those tender years."

His wife thinks a turning point came during his ministry in Weldon (1941-1946) when he witnessed the brutal treatment of a black person by a policeman. The victim was guilty of no offense other than being too near white folk at the local theatre entrance. She reports that Finlator came home outraged and vowing that he would no longer sit quietly and allow this kind of thing to go unchallenged.

From the start of his ministry he had sought an avenue to express his opinions to a wider audience. Taking pen in hand, he dashed off articles to the state Baptist paper, the *Biblical Recorder*. For the year 1940 alone he contributed twenty-four articles. While they were mostly literary flourishes, primarily homiletic and scarcely cognizant of the catastrophic events of the outside world, they were nonetheless sprinkled with some sharp social commentary. An early article carried the ominous title, "The Peril of Pulpit Freedom," (30 November 1938). On 22 May 1940 he raised for the first time the question of keeping the Negro "in his place." Close to Independence Day, in his 3 July column, he challenged blind patriotism and needless militarism. On 17 July he exposed the euphemism, "white supremacy." In a major article, "Safeguarding our Baptist Democracy," which was the first submitted in response to the editor's call for reader reaction to the Southern Baptist Convention's action at its Baltimore annual session, Finlator declared:

> But messengers to the Southern Baptist Convention seem to have only a favorable vote to the findings of their committees. This suggests a mock parliament in a totalitarian state whose only function is to rubber stamp official decrees.

He wondered aloud if Baptists were really afraid of their native polity—namely, participatory democracy.[7]

---

[7]Finlator, "Safeguarding Our Baptist Democracy," *Biblical Recorder* 106 (21 August 1940): 6.

Already in the early years of his public writings a certain tact
is detectable. The minister must cultivate the collective conscience. "Certainly, too, he must not shrink from sounding the
clarion note summoning the conscience of the people from its le-
thargic indifference to existing evils around and within," he wrote
on 30 November 1938 in the *Recorder*. And what are these evils
but social sins? In the issue of 17 August he had given some indication.

> For while we have in all conscience been loyal to the above
> [principles] we have gone on acquiring land in such a way as to
> perpetuate the low state of tenantry and share-cropping; we have
> kept subjugated, ignorant, and exploited a race, admittedly our
> equal, and in our own country from no choice of its own; we have
> erected great industrial plants and, until forced to do otherwise,
> have paid starvation wages to and imposed inhuman conditions
> upon our workers. We, the great American middle-class, the Ajax
> of the church, we Christians of a dwarfed Christianity have done,
> still are doing, all this with apparently no pangs of guilt, no abid-
> ing sense of injustice, complacent in the smugness of conformity
> to these uninstructed consciences and unexplained hearts.[8]

That was a rare voice in the midst of the acculturated religion of
Eastern North Carolina. Even Finlator confined these convictions to the pulpit and church press; he had not yet dared act out
his unconventional beliefs. Only twice during the war years did
his columns remind his readers that the very fascism America was
fighting abroad was in danger of being embraced at home. He did
initiate the removal of both the Christian flag and the American
flag from his sanctuary at the Weldon church, but he secretly
hoped nobody would notice.

With his transfer to the Elizabeth City First Baptist Church
in 1946, Finlator exhibited the first signs of moving beyond the
traditional preacher role. A lawyer member of the congregation
remembers how "every time he opened his mouth half the world
got mad." The local editor, Herbert Peele, soon commented on his
alarming impact. "I like to hear Finlator preach," Peele reported.

---

[8]Finlator, "The Christian Must Instruct His Conscience," *Biblical Recorder*
104 (17 August 1938): 1.

"He does not indulge in platitudes and he always gives me some-thing to think about. As a rule I also get hit."

But the things that brought him trouble during his ten-year tenure there were his actions on race, labor (unions for sawmill workers and the plight of migrant laborers), the gambling asso-ciated with the dog-racing track in Currituck County, and the World Council of Churches with its social agenda.

What little action Finlator took on the race question per-tained to his cooperation with the city black preachers, engage-ments at the local black college, and his prompt, forthright endorsement of the 1954 decision of the U. S. Supreme Court in *Brown v. Board of Education.* Far more telling were his ties with the Southern organizations that promoted equality and integra-tion. By far, his most radical extracurricular indulgence was as a founding member and editorial writer for the maverick Baptist publication, *Christian Frontiers.* In this journal, founded in 1946, he burst full bloom into a larger social context, apparently freed at last from ecclesiastical restraints. In its pages he hammered away at the value of unions, the dangers of militarism, the ne-cessity of ecumenicity, and similarly controversial issues. His congregation soon became aware they had a different brand of Baptist preacher. He recalls that "the *Christian Frontiers* expe-rience served to liberate me. It was a daring, bracing, challeng-ing venture and of course I was never the same thereafter."

Crucial to the formation of the journal was the reality that the *Recorder,* under new editorship and sensitive to Finlator's in-creasing distance from ordinary Baptist readers, no longer wel-comed his voluminous submissions. So it is not surprising that in an article submitted but now rejected, in November 1953, he pin-pointed his new dilemma.

> The gracious editor of this journal often chides me for writing too frequently along controversial lines and suggests that I turn my pen to themes of a more devotional nature. . . . We Baptists are a people not of creeds but of liberty, and our basis of cooper-ation is not of conformism but of voluntarism. Lovers and res-pecters of free conscience our unity is in our very diversity. We are not afraid of truth from whatever source and we are not afraid of error, given a chance in the open forum of free discussion to

combat error. But we are afraid of fear itself, of creeping rigidity
of thought, of the want of self-confidence that expresses itself in
investigating committees and discourtesy.

As for his relation with unions, Finlator had never kept secret
his admiration for what unions had done in developing America
and for the improvement of laboring conditions. His own father
had been a member of the railroad union. Locally a strike occurred among the sawmill workers. The manager of the plant was
a member of Finlator's church, but Finlator lent support to the
strikers. As for the local agricultural migrant workers, Finlator
made a discovery that would stick with him for the remainder of
his life. Years later, in 1967, addressing a Congressional committee investigating their plight, he described to its members his
early awakening.

> Naturally, being located where I was I felt for the migrants.
> Through this area each spring there passed one of the main-
> streams of migrant labor. There I saw at first hand their terrible
> plight. No one then, and very few now, seem responsible for their
> welfare and for their environmental decency. The churches in our
> area did a little but mostly in the nature of palliatives. I tried to
> arouse public indignation and compassion, but was not too suc-
> cessful.

As for Finlator's actions with regard to the dog racing track
at Moyock and the World Council of Churches, Willard Savin, a
member of the church, has written an inside view.

> One Saturday morning our pastor, who was seeking ways to
> cause closure of the dog track, called Charlie Vann and myself to
> his office. He told of his activities in pursuit of his goal. He said
> we must get this issue into the courts and prove the dog track to
> be illegal. But in order to get the case to court, some citizens have
> to be arrested for placing bets. In other words, he was proposing
> a test case. He said defense lawyers were ready and one of them
> was waiting downtown now to talk. "Will you allow yourselves
> to be arrested at the dog track for gambling?" Then he added, "I
> myself would get arrested but my wife won't let me." Charlie and
> I squirmed and listened politely but we declined.[9]

---

[9]Willard Savin to McLeod Bryan, 23 September 1981.

That a Baptist preacher could urge his deacons to get arrested for gambling reveals a great deal about the new parameters of Finlator's behavior! Mr. Savin also describes the trouble within the congregation over its affiliation with the World Council of Churches.

> A few months prior to Bill's leaving our pastorate, the Chairman of the Diaconate brought to our attention that our church by action of the pastor was a member of the World Council of Churches. Many of our members believed this organization to be advocating revolutionary methods, including racial disturbance, in attempting to achieve whatever they believed in. This diaconate session was a very stormy meeting as Mr. Finlator was brought to task, if I may use that expression, for having caused our church to be affiliated. The deacons voted for us to terminate our membership.[10]

Some observers have seen his time in the Elizabeth City Church as a training ground for Finlator's more radical and aggressive social action thereafter. Its membership deserves a great deal of credit for tolerating his early experiments in social change. By 1956, when he was called by the Pullen Memorial Baptist Church in Raleigh, his reputation for controversy was well-honed. In turn, Pullen had established its own unique reputation, that of a free pulpit under a series of free-wheeling pastors. The fortunate coincidence that brought pastor and congregation together may be gathered from the introduction given Finlator by attorney Alex Dennison before the Wake County Bar Association, 4 February 1970.

> In a sense, Finlator is not unlike a lawyer. Underlying our advocacy system is the basic belief that by having both sides of an issue forcefully presented before an impartial arbiter, justice will be reached. I think he believes that by presenting a minority, sometimes shocking point of view, he will cause us to more carefully study the position we have taken and thereby arrive at a more well-founded position. He believes that the church should not be restricted to quietly ladling out comfort and compassion

---

[10]Ibid.

and promise of serenity on Sunday mornings completely aloof
from the turmoil of civic issues. He believes that the church has
an obligation to take part in examining important issues and
providing leadership in arriving at sound, moral judgments on
those issues. He believes that if the attorney general is the
watchdog of the public purse, then the church should be the
watchdog of the public conscience. . . . Despite the ringing assur-
ances in our constitution about freedom of speech, such freedom
cannot often really be found—not because of any deficiency in our
laws, but because of deficiencies in our people. People are not tol-
erant of forceful expression of ideas contrary to their own. But I
am proud to say that our preacher can, and that he wants to.

His critics thought Finlator and Pullen deserved each other;
but other people considered their marriage a dream match. It had
all the drama of the ancient story of the young rabbi returning to
the synagogue in his hometown of Nazareth, without, of course,
the tragedy of the Gospel—the hometown boy makes good and re-
turns to make the hometown more distinguished. The facts are,
however, that there was never a time without some apprehension
within the congregation, and ultimately his tenure was to be cut
short by a "forced" early retirement. "I suppose to some extent I
lived in a kind of dream world," Finlator admitted in the aftermath of that controversial event.

> I subjected these wonderful people to a whole lot and it is little
> short of miraculous that they sustained, if not tolerated, me for
> more than a quarter of a century. I know of few other churches
> in the South where I might have survived under similar circum-
> stances. There's never been a time that a minister as kooky as I
> am hasn't distressed them. But the Pullen folk are the most free-
> will Baptists I've ever seen. They are a fascinating collection of
> humanity. They did their own thinking. This is what made them
> the most exciting congregation I ever knew.

His very first year was not without its critical anonymous note:
"We, a large group of Pullen Church, wish to reprimand you severely for your pro-NAACP stand and your general stupidity relative to this problem." A visitor to the church on 10 March 1977
left him a poem.

Pullen stands for preachers who in
politics dabble
Exciting the fury and hate of the rabble,
Enflaming the mind with fanatical vigor
To crush down the whites and build up
the nigger.

Nonetheless, members of the Pullen congregation usually backed Finlator's varied campaigns, sometimes suffering ugly smears, and together they braved common foes. Most notably they resisted the denomination's designation as "differing churches"— only eleven, of which Pullen was one—of congregations that accepted members baptized by other Christian commmunions. Pullen stood its ground before the Convention's investigating committee in 1973, and defended its practice as fully Christian and in line with the autonomy principle of the local Baptist congregation. Finlator tried extra hard to fulfill all of his pastoral duties, but as more and more demands compelled him to divide his time between churchly duties and community service, as his name made the headlines all too frequently, as he took sides and expounded opinions not always supported by the congregation— all in the church's name—Finlator was obliged to defend his behavior. "I did try to warn my congregation," he recalls,

> that all the "noise and fireworks of controversy" and my understanding and assessment of it is not the same as the "voice of God." I have never claimed any inerrancy or insisted that I have a special pipeline to heaven unavailable to others. I did indeed pop off too many times and I have been biased from time to time. Issues before our people today are complex and convoluted and it is not right for a minister to give easy solutions. We just have to be on our guard continually against this.

In a sermon on 29 October 1978 he explained "Why I Joined Them." After listing but a few of the countless organizations he served, he argued

> that my involvement with other groups stems from biblical and theological commitment with my [Baptist] church and faith. . . . Please note that these organizations promise me no economic reward or political preferment. I am not looking for a job. I have a

glorious one. . . . I point out to you, however, that the smaller groups particularly are unselfish, that they exist for the cause of others, that we could write over each of them the Latin phrase "pro humanitate." Please note that the words "friend" and "justice" and "liberty" and "rights" are the big words in the titles and are full of challenge and hope.

All the time Finlator was busy in these wider humanitarian causes, he was a full-time pastor—visiting the sick, marrying the young, burying the dead, "keeping church." Pullen graciously shared him for his two-pronged ministry. Furthermore, the church sheltered many members, who, disaffected with their own Baptist and other denominational congregations and eager to be advocates for applied Christianity, had gravitated there. Also within its very halls many liberal organizations found a home when other doors were shut to them. The state chapter of the Civil Liberties union was chartered there; so was the North Carolina organization opposing capital punishment. Both the National Organization for Women and the Equal Rights Amendment sponsors found hospitality there—the state chairwoman for the ERA was a member. Often the North Carolina Advisory Committee on Civil Rights convened in its rooms.

In accepting the position at Pullen Finlator had envisioned just such a springboard for larger involvement. Writing to a friend after accepting the pulpit, on 10 July 1956, he shared his enthusiasm.

> As you know it is no easy assignment trying to follow in the steps of Poteat. The quality and kindness of members will keep me from being terrified. . . . [But] this pulpit is to me a great challenge. In all frankness I would rather be pastor of this church than any other in North Carolina, than anywhere in the South.

Celebrating his twentieth anniversary, he could still say that "While my words and actions over the years caused a number of our fellowship to leave us—and they have left on principle and remained good friends—I would like to say to you and to the world that not once has this church officially censored me or offered the remotest suggestion that could be interpreted as diminishing the freedom of pulpit and pastor."

Yet within three years of those words, in 1979, powerful members of the congregation, headed by the Board of Deacons, put pressure on Finlator to retire. After twenty-three years the dream had burst. Pullen, which for nearly a century had established itself as the spiritual haven for persons searching for some local congregation taking the Gospel seriously, and which prided itself on its pulpit, the freest of the free, found itself at loggerheads with its controversial preacher. Heretofore, where disagreement was healthy and honestly bandied about, was openly confronted and rationally settled, there was now a break in communications.

The ostensible cause for the row was Finlator's 23 March 1979 telegram to President Jimmy Carter urging him to expedite the executive procedures to desegregate completely the university system of North Carolina. He had sent the telegram as chairman of the North Carolina Advisory Committee on Civil Rights. However, before that moment, there had been signs of ambivalence in the relationship between Finlator and the Pullen church. Some in the membership had felt that Finlator was too one-sided in his advocacy, that he often went too far and too fast, and that he should more carefully dissociate his controversial leadership in the public sector from his affiliation with Pullen. That some resentment had long lain dormant is obvious from excerpts from letters of two long-term members.

> I believe you, and other Pullen leaders historically, have emphasized "aspects of social living" too much to the neglect of individual and personal living. By and large, it has been my experience that the preaching ministry has neglected to inspire, to nurture, to support and to lead me in personal and spiritual growth.

> I do enjoy seminars and clever discussions, but I go to the eleven o'clock worship service to renew the spiritual aspect of my being. For the sermon to ignore that part of me leaves me feeling quite unfulfilled and even angry. . . . An intellectual discussion that says nothing to the personal lives of the members of the congregation is not my idea of an appropriate sermon.

More specific letters blamed Finlator for sending the telegram per se. One member wrote 27 March 1979,

This is not the leadership I respect, desire or follow in our church. It is not in the paths of reconciliation preached upon. It is an extreme disservice to the responsible educational leadership of our State, our friends and Pullen Memorial Church. I weary in apology for this type expression from one of our ministers. It does not appear to me a logical or essential extension of a free pulpit. It is more an abuse of privilege of association.

Another member wrote on 4 April 1979,

Again I beg for an explanation of the reasons for such drastic action. This is an unpleasant undertaking for me. . . . I have always cherished belonging to a church that practices freedom of speech by its members, but freedom of speech carries with it an equal amount of responsibility. I do not think we have a right to irresponsibly yell "fire" in a crowded theatre just for publicity purposes. This, I regret to way, is what I think you have done. Frankly, I am greatly saddened and dismayed by your unprecedented action.

The wonder is that the "dream match" lasted as long as it did. Often the tension brought on by the daring claims of a free pulpit is too much for the institutional church. The possibility of such a collision was not unforeseen by both Pullen and Finlator. Just a couple of months before inviting Finlator as its new pastor, the church had formulated a job description that reads in part:

A free pulpit. As in the past we want our pastor to be free to interpret the Christian message for ourselves and the world as he sees it.

A challenging message. Our fellowship will always demand sermons which are thoughtfully planned and which are distinctly related to the current problems facing Christian bodies over the world today.

Summary. We desire to bear our own testimony in our own way in this community and to avoid an unthinking following for mass programs. This challenge which is ours at Pullen must also be his who will serve as our minister.

Likewise for Finlator the free pulpit was the critical element in his own ministry. In an address on the subject in 1958 he declared,

The miracle of change, the leaven of transfiguration, begins to take place in the community where there is at least one free voice in one free church. The editor, the school teacher, yes, even the politician, breathe a freer air and move with a firmer courage, however unconsciously, and act with a different emphasis in those communities where truth is constantly being proclaimed. Truth spoken in one area elicits the expression of truth in every area. All other freedoms depend ultimately upon freedom of religion and the freedom of religion is null and void until the pulpit has come to speak the truth in love.

Scholarly observers of the Southern scene often commented on the uniqueness of the pairing of Pullen and Finlator. Professor Shelton Smith of Duke Divinity School wrote to Finlator on 30 March 1976, "Your Pullen Memorial ministry always strikes me as extraordinary. How have you managed to be so prophetical and successful in a denomination and region that is, on the whole, so amazingly conservative?" Professor Edward Pruden, formerly of the First Baptist Church in Washington, D.C. and later a member of the faculty at Southeastern Baptist Theological Seminary, wrote on 12 March 1975, "You represent many outside your own congregation when you take a stand for good causes, and we are all proud of you."

However well the Pullen Church managed to preserve its image over the long tenure of Finlator's ministry crowded with antics severely testing its guarantee of a free pulpit, that fell apart with the division within the membership in the aftermath of the 1979 telegram. For a year and a half the dispute raged on until Finlator announced on 24 August 1980 his coming retirement in 1982. The sharply contrasting appraisals of the Finlator phenomenon that had been widely aired outside the church for years now descended upon the membership itself. As early as 17 May 1969 a reader's letter to the *Recorder* had documented the hostility at large.

I find Mr. Finlator offensive in that he has given the general public a bad image of the Baptist denomination, its people and religion. I have been told by many people in and out of the Baptist denomination that if I could explain Mr. Finlator—a lot of

people would like to hear me. I cannot explain Mr. Finlator, can
you?

Even earlier a personal attack on him had appeared in the letters
column of the *News and Observer,* on 15 December 1964.

> Rev. Finlator, Raleigh liberal Baptist preacher and do-gooder,
> has popped off again. Some of the pain in his stomach may be re-
> lieved but no cubic inches have been added to his stature. In as
> much as he seems troubled about images possibly he ought to look
> in his own mirror because the image many people see of this
> preacher is of one more interested in seeking publicity than in
> preaching the gospel to the broken hearted.
>
> Baptists have always been a peculiar people practicing
> strange beliefs for which they have bared their backs to the lash.
> Non-conforming fundamental beliefs have made Baptist people
> great and prosperous. This layman comes out of four generations
> of Southern Baptists, but Rev. Finlator is not the kind of Baptist
> I was raised on, and there is some indication to the effect that he
> is completely out of step with today's Southern Baptists. Wonder
> why he doesn't switch brands more to his liking.

Sometimes these personal attacks could be brutal. For the sake
of the writer, one letter of 26 March 1979 will be allowed to remain anonymous.

> Finlator, you are a disgrace to the white race. The reason this
> country is in the mess it is is due to you and your kind. You are
> nothing but a professional agitator and publicity seeker and
> should be sent to Russia.

Yet throughout the final dispute Finlator seemed to be wor-
ried more about the possible damage to Pullen's reputation than
about his own loss. In a "town meeting" the congregation staged
to air all sides, Finlator himself took the floor to address Pullen's
noble tradition.

> As one of that increasingly rare breed who grew up on the
> sidewalks of Raleigh, I have followed the history of Pullen Me-
> morial with special interest, always aware, even from high school
> years, that it was a special fellowship. . . . My strongest impres-

sion in retrospect is one of courage and decisiveness that Pullen people seem always to have possessed.

He continued to list one by one the victories of the past as the congregation overcame cultural and denominational restrictions. He cited its ecumenical spirit in its affiliation with the North Carolina Council of Churches and the American Baptist Convention. He cited its inclusiveness, which had undergirded the rewriting of its constitution in 1958, before almost any other Baptist church, to include "any person" (Finlator explained that "this word was used to include all races")in its membership. "Yet another instance of Pullen decisiveness," he added, "occurred when our fellow Baptists were up in arms against our practice of receiving Christians into our church without requiring immersion. They wanted to oust us or, as they put it, to withdraw fellowship from us." During that "town meeting" member after member extolled Pullen's singular record. One of the best statements came from Jon Lindsey.

> One of the "givens" of Pullen is that it is a congregation which has for a variety of reasons established a heritage which places it outside the mainstream of "Southern Baptist" traditions as well as "American Baptist" traditions. It has tried to establish a tradition of independence, sometimes without clearly being aware of the price, nor the responsibilities. . . . The heritage of Pullen is what attracted me to the congregation, like it has attracted most of the rest of the members. That heritage is the continual attempt to synthesize the best of denominationalism and the total heritage of Christianity into a viable faith expression for the historical period.

Most of the speeches made were in the pastor's defense and dozens of letters reached the Board of Deacons pleading with them to reconsider the date for Finlator's retirement. Typical of the vast majority of the letters received by the Board are one from a well-known journalist and another from a professor at North Carolina State University, both members of Pullen.

> Members of Pullen should keep in mind a number of factors as they decide the fate of Bill Finlator. Number One. It will be a debilitating experience and the effects will be felt for years.

Number Two. The image of Pullen will be damaged. If Finlator
is forced out, where will the applause come from? Because Pullen
has such a distinctive church, in the south as well as in the state,
attention is going to be focused on what is done here. The image
of Pullen is important. I first became aware of it in 1938, while a
student at Wake Forest. This image has been forged by ministers
with special qualities who were supported by an independent
congregation of educated people. . . . We read about what is happening in the Southern Baptist Convention. The ultraconserva-
tives are taking over; throats are being cut, but prayerfully. The
doctrinal dictators are assuming command. To all of this add the
news that Pullen Memorial Baptist Church, the ancient symbol
of opposition to this kind of thing, is giving the boot to its minister. Great will be the joy in the convention hierarchy.

First of all, our "free pulpit" has made possible a prophetic
ministry that has earned for our church respect if not agreement
from individuals and institutions far beyond the geographical
area it serves. This freedom has enabled our ministers to look at
a variety of issues, denominational, social, educational, international, or local from a viewpoint that has stood in sharp and
refreshing contrast with prevailing miasmas of Southern orthodoxy and regional chauvinism. Please consider how unfavorably
this action may reflect on the Church. Would a man of like promise come to lead us knowing that we had forced out an able servant because of an unpopular stand or age? I think our reputation
as a "liberal" church is at stake here.

This was one controversy Finlator did not enjoy. However
graciously he acted by retiring 30 June 1982 and by not granting
any of his customary press interviews to present his own account
of the events or his own feelings, it was accepted that neither he
nor the victors enjoyed it

Next to the issue of his forced retirement nothing shook Finlator more than the discovery of his FBI file and the knowledge
that the government had kept him under surveillance. He had
dedicated his life to extolling the virtues of Americanism. He had
lived what he thought was an exemplary life morally as a Baptist
preacher. He was as thoroughly a native-born, loyal citizen as he
could imagine. His life had been an open book; he had done nothing secretive or subversive. "Why, then," he reflected with aston-

ishment when he made the discovery, "did they have to pick on me?" In the light of the common knowledge of the FBI's harassment of Martin Luther King, Jr., he was certainly not unaware of the department's questionable practices, and he had even tried to alert the public to the dangers of the department's enlarging powers.

The very difficulty he encountered in securing his file under the Freedom of Information Act bothered him. In the fall of 1981 he mailed his first request. In its reply the FBI denied having any file on him. After one and a half years of further inquiry, they finally admitted to some data. Meanwhile the congressional offices of Representatives Stephen Neal and Ike Andrews were asked to intervene in securing the file. On 31 January 1983 what sections of the file the Washington office chose to release arrived. According to the covering letter, "110 pages were reviewed and six pages withheld in their entirety." Only the records of the D. C. office were handed over, and of that material about one-half was censored.

On inspection of the file, two conclusions were obvious to Finlator. First, the entire coverage of his surveillance seemed lacking; the reports covered only the years 1948 to 1972. Second, the condition of the file after censoring and the incompetent reporting of field agents gave a distorted picture of the true facts. Much of the data was based on newspaper clippings, accusing innuendos of right-wing columnists, and hearsay evidence. Not a single item quoted a balanced or positive evaluation of Finlator's character and actions. One report from the Charlotte office, dated 26 April 1963, did not even bother to check the proper name of his church. Twice it was listed as "the *Poland* Memorial Baptist Church." The FBI had considered Finlator's opposition to segregation subversive. A quote from the *Charlotte News* pertained to a speech in which Finlator said, "Segregation is dead. It is as dead as a door nail." An agent reporting on the first Vietnam Moratorium day, 15 October 1969 in Salem Square, where Finlator was one of several speakers, mentioned "an acid rock band"—the very last thing imaginable on the hallowed ground of this Moravian stronghold. Even something as harmless as his letter to U. S. Attorney General Nicholas Katzenbach, dated 7 July 1965, which said no more than "Please let me urge the Department of Justice to withhold all further prosecutions under the Internal Security Act awaiting the outcome of a case bearing on its constitutionality" found its way to the files by 20 July. Moreover, from the notations on the sequential reports it was clear that these twisted and dubious appraisals were given widespread circulation. Typical is this notation at the top of the report for 12 December 1967: "Copies being disseminated locally to military intelligence, secret service, and USA's at Raleigh and Greensboro."

This imagined threat to the internal security of the nation was none other than a native North Carolina Baptist preacher. Few American citizens could have more solid and bona fide credentials. If any good accrued from the release of the files it had nothing to do with clearing Finlator's name—that was obvious without the necessity of secret police snooping. When one compares the triviality of the material in the FBI files with the massive collection of public documentation on Finlator's career stored presently at the Wisconsin Historical Society, the North Carolina Archives, and the Duke University Library with its Finlator Civil Liberties holdings, the FBI file pales into insignificance, even insult. A review of the file gives the impression that the reporting agents were "straining at gnats" in an attempt to make a case against Finlator. And if the blacked-out material in his released files was designed to protect the other persons named (as the Department's covering letter alleged), then, judging by the quality and accuracy of the reports on Finlator, they had nothing to worry about.

Finlator, one of the staunchest defenders of the American system, could hardly bring himself to admit his own victimization. He hardly conceived of himself as a threat to America, "an enemy of the people." He had with abandon exercised a freedom of speech and association under the aegis of the Bill of Rights that he so ardently loved, and for so doing had found himself targeted as a "disloyal" citizen.

Finlator regarded himself foremost as a Baptist preacher. "Your honors, I am a humble Baptist preacher"—these were the words with which he opened many a speech in the halls of government, labor, business and academia. He was not ashamed of his calling or of his Baptist affiliation. "I am primarily a Baptist minister serving my church. I'm not a reformer, or a radical, or a professional do-gooder, in spite of the rumors." One might add that he loved his denomination so much that he worked to add dignity and distinction to its name. Throughout his stormy career he remained absolutely devoted—a Baptist with a vengeance, some would say. At times he could give the impression that he unduly thought of himself as the last remaining true Baptist. He constantly reminded his brothers and sisters how radical their heritage is. His devotion, however, depicted a lover's quarrel. He minced no words in describing his denomination as "provincial and somewhat parochial."

That his love was not always reciprocated is hardly surprising. The attitude of his fellow Baptists toward him was, to say the least, ambivalent. They nominally accepted him along with the other mavericks the communion seemed to attract, but official recognition was generally withheld. There was little appreciation for his controversial witness. That Baptists were reluctant to give him any power, any office, any recognition, was understandable to him in the light of his needling them, but nonetheless it remained a point of sorrow for him. His theology had built into itself just such a rejection as a normal reaction to the Gospel's stringent mandates. And although absolutely devoted to the institutional church, he realized that "the church devils are the worse devils." While honors and rewards were clearly not among his goals, he had received a good number in the closing years of his career. He was awarded a doctorate by his alma mater (1973), the Frank P. Graham Award of the ACLU (1980), and a citation from the North Carolina AFL-CIO (1981). A section of the Duke University Library had been named for him (1983). Secular awards he was to receive in bountiful supply, but the religious community to which he had devoted his entire professional career apparently still viewed him with suspicion. A clear example of this was the official Baptist refusal to join in sponsoring a two-day seminar honoring Finlator by focusing on the issues of his public career, entitled "Religion and the Humane Society." It was conducted in September 1982 and received abundant sponsorship and attendance from all over the South and the nation in its sessions on the Wake Forest University campus. The state Christian Life Committee, for which Finlator had provided perhaps the most brilliant model for longer than any other Baptist, turned a deaf ear to the invitation. Finlator could hardly ignore these signals of rejection.

While Finlator relished controversy and generally took it in stride, there were times he felt lonely and hurt. In a letter to Glen Archer on 5 September 1967, he confessed "that I live in an island alone without friends." To John Baerlin on 20 April 1970 he wrote, "These are not easy times at all to be alive and sometimes I have the temptation of running away and hiding." He clearly had reasons to be depressed and even fearful for his life, since he often threw himself into tense and dangerous positions. There were the usual hate letters, obscene phone calls late at night, an occasional threat on his life. He went so far as to park his car under the street lamp just in case. But his worry was more about his family. "There were indeed moments of personal fear," he said once. But, he added,

> Perhaps greater than this was the sense of guilt, the fear that somebody might take something out on one of my children. Just how much my wife and family suffered is something I am not able to compute. Probably the children went through more in their teen ages than we'll ever know, though they seem to have come through pretty unscathed. Perhaps a minister's wife who has this additional burden of a husband like me, suffers most, especially when the guns attack both inside and outside the church. I think it may be safely said that the family has felt we stood on the ground of principles and are proud to have done so.

Finlator shared his own apprehension with his son Wallace in a letter on the day following the assassination of Dr. Martin Luther King, Jr.

> You don't need any advice from me but you may like to know that one of my Negro professor friends invited me to go on the Shaw campus with him when the students were shouting and hurling epithets and articles. I told him, out of fear, that a white face would be a handicap even with his proffered protection. As a matter of fact, I was also afraid and I left.

As a central figure in many heated controversies, Finlator could have been a marked man. This was the decade of assassinations. A member of his church, having just watched him attack capital punishment on a television talk show and dating her letter "midnight, March 20, 1975," shared her solicitude.

> But, Sir, I am concerned. There are all sorts of people who, being passionately *for* something like capital punishment, will be even more passionately *against* those whose ideas cross-up their own. Do be careful.
>
> Strangely—or is it—they don't seem to "do-in" the crooked, the underhanded, the schemers, the devious, the cruel—just those with whom they get "religiously" angry: Martin Luther King, John Kennedy, Robert Kennedy, Lincoln, Jesus.
>
> You will act as you feel you must. No doubt I am being selfish, but it has never seemed smart to me to let yourself get killed. It leaves too much that has to be done.
>
> Maybe what I am really wanting to say is: I am afraid for you; those rabid haters are not worth it—they're not going to change—and don't let anything happen to you—for your sake, your family's sake, our sake and for the things you can yet help bring about."

Finlator had to endure many uncomplimentary epithets— "Comrade Finlator," "nigger lover," "pink preacher," "traitor," "professional agitator." Inwardly he was deeply hurt when people misread him. "I am not by constitution a tough-skinned person. I am deeply sensitive to such brutal remarks. But I have tried not take them personally, managing a smile and brushing them off with a joke." A good example of his resiliency, which accompanied his life-style of gentility, personableness and prompt forgiveness, occurred when he was participating in a civil rights demonstration in Raleigh. Charlie Craven, a reporter for the *News and Observer,* was standing on the sidewalk interviewing Finlator. As a passer-by looked Finlator straight in the face, he taunted, "You s.o.b.!" Finlator instantly turned to Craven and quipped, "Did you hear what that man called you?"

Worse than the threat of physical harm was the actual loss of friends, the public ostracism, the closing of doors to dialogue, and the loss of opportunities to speak. He had to face squarely this risk and balance it against any prospective positive results that might come from his outspokenness.

> I have known that I was a voice in the wilderness and I would not be able to persuade any substantial number of my fellow citizens, even among the clergy, to join my causes. This is a price one must be willing and even happy to pay. But there is always this other consideration. No person can try to listen carefully to the gospel and be aware of the world today without becoming controversial. When push comes to shove, I'd rather be with the non-silent ones. I console myself that Christ was a trouble-maker.

Much of Finlator's controversial image derived from his "consorting with" marginal people: the poor, the imprisoned, the petitioners, the minorities, the unconventional, the labor organizers, the draft protesters, the women's libbers, the civil rights marchers, and even an occasional communist, revolutionary, anarchist and professional agitator. His church office was open to these people, his ear was sympathetic to their pleas, and word soon circulated as to his availability. Yet, on the other hand, he looked upon himself as "something of a Last Puritan." "Believe it or not," he would say, "I am basically conservative. Look at my life, a thoroughly institutional man, a Democrat, a supporter of law and order, with middle-class standards." He actually penned an article entitled, "Why I Am a Conservative," which was reprinted in several journals in 1976. In it he elaborated his conservatism in five areas: the Bible, Baptist polity, the Constitution, the good earth, and education.

> First, I am a strict constructionist, which, I understand, is a hallmark of the true conservative. That's the way I take the ethical teachings of Jesus, at face value. . . . Secondly, a strict construction of any of these [Baptist] tenets gets you immediately in trouble today. Take the matter of the free conscience. During the war in Vietnam it was unthinkable to most of our Baptist leadership that there was any other choice than blindly to support the policies of the government. Dissent or protest was little short of treason. Yet Baptists are people whose founders protested the endless wars of the European nations and in many cases refused to serve in the military. . . . [Third] In politics too, I am a strict

constructionist. . . . Politically I live and move and have my being in the spirit and letter of the Declaration of Independence, the Constitution, the Bill of Rights, the Gettysburg Address, and the Second Inaugural Address of Abraham Lincoln. . . . I am a conservative in the fourth place because I am a conservationist. . . . A final and brief word about my conservatism has to do with education. . . . So put me down as a conservative in religion. I want to know more about the faith of our fathers. Put me down as a conservative in government. I want to be steeped in the sacred lore of our nation. Put me down as a conservative who wants to conserve and restore what is left of our natural resources. Put me down as a conservative in education.

In embracing conservatism, Finlator caught the public—particularly his opponents—off guard. However, his enemies hardly shared his interpretation of the concept. If they had looked more closely at his social philosophy, they would have discerned that his so-called radicalism did not go very far. For instance, he was as wary of communism as other Americans were. A case in point is the record of his dealings with the Southern Conference for Human Welfare. Headquartered in New Orleans, its president was Aubrey Williams, its vice-president Benjamin Mays, and James Dombrowski its Director. Finlator was a quite active early member when SCHW began in the 1930s, and he eventually joined its board of directors. In a letter of 25 August 1948, however, he withdrew his name from the board.

> I regret deeply to have to write this letter. . . . I do not think that I am a victim of the current frenzy, I might even say manipulated frenzy, over communism that is sweeping away the sanity of our people. But because of recent exposures that have come to me elsewhere than Washington [where a Congressional hearing appeared to have uncovered some communist connections]. . . . I am led to the necessity of severing my ties with the Conference. Sufficient knowledge has come to light to make incredible any belief that the Conference—as Heaven knows it ought to have been—was a grass roots affair, indigenous to the South.

It appears that the burden of his decision rested on the question whether radical change is imposed from the outside or originates from within, from Southerners able to transcend their own limitations. This would have been in line with his maxim that true conservatism should be able to produce its own radicality. When the SCHW reorganized after this investigation, becoming the Southern Conference Educational Fund, Finlator continued as a leader in it.

Another instance of his moderation is his change of stance vis-à-vis traditional Southern Protestantism's anti-Catholicism. Very early, in an article in the *Recorder,* 14 March 1945, while readily admitting the possibility of playing on religious prejudice, he had affirmed that "the Roman Church is out to get America." He described Catholics as persons "taught to feel alike, believe alike and vote alike," and the Church as a body that "has taken advantage of general Protestant tolerance." Such extremism could not withstand his many subsequent encounters with individual Catholics in social causes and his growing ecumenical-mindedness. By the end of his career he had several bishops as friends (Bishop Gossman spoke at his retirement ceremony), and he gave the ACLU speech of 1983 honoring a Catholic priest for his civil libertarianism.

The Pullen Church had been closely associated with Protestants and Other Americans United. Finlator offended some members by withdrawing from its national board of directors. That his move was not easy is manifest in his letter of 5 September 1967 to Glen Archer, the executive director and his personal friend.

> I think that there may still be a very valid mission for P.O.A.U. Today the real threat to separation of church and state is no longer the Roman Catholic Church but rather it is the religion of Americanism. . . . This means that the country which began espousing a separation of church and state doctrine has now, in many ways, itself become a religion with its priests and fanatics and unAmerican activities committees, etc. At this point dissent with administration policy may be the same as heresy some years ago, religious heresy, that is. Do you not feel what I am saying? Is there no way POAU can make known to people that ours is still a religiously neutral government and they do it great disservice who invest it with the sanctity of faith.

Finlator's "radicalness" now consisted in holding the conservative Catholic Church as an ally against a new form of idolatry, statism.

What made Finlator's social position so hard to pin down was his fluctuation between romanticism and realism. Realistically, he found himself at odds with his closest compatriots when they became too doctrinaire, when the liberal cause took priority over other considerations, and when winning at any price was the accepted goal. They, in turn, often thought him naive. He did possess a Don Quixote tendency to take off after any whirling windmill. On the romantic side, Finlator could be a dedicator of gardens (as at Tryon Palace), the lover of poetry (as in the Sir Walter Raleigh tribute), the promoter of libraries (a member of Friends of the Library), and sports enthusiast (he actually gave an invocation at the Hot Stove League). But he was also the tough-minded realist, able to hold his own in the toughest negotiations, yielding not an inch in debate, never expecting utopian results while pressing for a whole loaf, yet amicably accepting a half loaf—or as he admitted to a friend, more often settling for a "quarter loaf."

Even so, his heroes for the long haul were more the "fools for Christ" variety. Jesus, Luther, Roger Williams, and his living idol, Frank Porter Graham. They were all united in being unusually transparent and buoyant, indeed a little naive. None of them fitted in an age of bureaucratic camouflage, nor did their success depend upon the image-making of public relations teams. Perhaps Finlator's best self-portrayal of his own controversial life is contained in his 1972 eulogy for Frank Graham.

> My final memory is a legacy. It has to do with Dr. Graham's attitude regarding controversy. How could so saintly a man be so controversial, and survive? It was always a part of my teaching that good men managed to avoid controversy but here was without doubt one of the most moral men who ever lived in our state moving from one controversy to the other and always maintaining respect and regard for his opponents. His formula was simple: Don't go around looking for controversy, mounted and armed like a knight. And don't waste your energies and resources on side issues and peripheral matters. But when you encounter situa-

tions of principle, when you are face to face with ethical issues, summon all your powers and meet them head on. He told us this and something else too. In a day when, as a famous football coach once put it, "Winning is not everything. It is the only thing," Dr. Graham said that losing may be more important than winning if you can make a witness in losing a battle. Be sure, he said, that you go down with all flags flying.

The best tribute to Finlator's own controversial labors comes from North Carolina's leading playwright, Paul Green, who like Graham had been a companion with Finlator in some of the tough battles. He wrote to Finlator on 12 November 1980, just a few days before his own death.

> Dreams that often get fastened down in steel and concrete, ritual and rote may prove obdurate and evil, cruel and oppressive, but we must keep at the business of awakening the sleeper, mustn't we? You do!

Chapter Three

CULTIVATING
THE PRESS AND LABOR

A FAVORITE JOKE ABOUT FINLATOR was that his Pullen congregation "could not come nigh unto him for the press," a play on Mark 2:4 (KJV). The press in turn felt that Finlator pressured the media for publicity. Editor Claud Sitton of the Raleigh *News and Observer,* speaking at the ceremony for Finlator's retirement, remarked that "Finlator is ready to pick up any tools at hand in pursuing his extended ministry and that includes the press. When a story broke on which he wished to be heard, you never had to worry about finding Bill: he had already found you."

Over the years Finlator received so much media coverage that some of his preacher peers complained. "The way you newspeople respond to Finlator you'd think there were no other sermons preached in North Carolina on a given Sunday," one wrote to an editor. Typical of that kind of criticism is a letter to the editor of the *News and Observer.*

Instead of quoting the Rev. W. W. Finlator every time some
issue of religious nature is in the news, why not allow your reporter to go out to [other churches]? Is it because you are certain
Finlator's remarks will be in line with your thinking and will in
all probability bolster your socialistic image? Your readers de-
serve to hear both sides of the matter, and we do want to be honest, fair and unbiased about this business of reporting the news,
don't we?[1]

Finlator did receive heavy coverage in both state and South-
wide papers and often by national wire services. Later in life he
was in demand on nationally televised talk shows. He was a col-
orful public figure; he was newsworthy. But his success with the
media has another explanation. As editor Sitton pinpointed it,
"Bill's success lies in his well-honed sense of what is topical, what
is interesting, what is important." Newsgatherers have become
so accustomed to religious charlatans begging for, stunting for and
buying headlines that they shy away from religion. They seemed
to find in Finlator an exception. The roster of cub reporters who
cut their journalistic teeth on this bone of contention called Finlator would name the veterans of the fourth estate within North
Carolina—Herbert O'Keefe, Sam Ragan, Jim Jenkins, Joe Doster, Roy Parker, Jr., Lloyd Preslar, Tom Lassiter, Virtie Stroup,
Bryan Haislip, Cole Campbell, to cite some who have published
profiles of Finlator over the years.

Whatever the basis, from his earliest days in the ministry
Finlator and the people of the press hit it off together. Theirs was
a mutual affection and they promoted each other. For his part,
Finlator rarely missed an opportunity to plug the freedom of the
press and to denounce censorship. David Milligan, an editor of a
remote paper in North Carolina, *Hyde News,* wrote to him on 6
September 1973.

I have a strong feeling that a hundred years from now your
name will be remembered as a great man who saw the Truth and
tried to cut a path along the way. . . . What a magnificent ex-

---

[1]Letter to the Editor, *News and Observer* (Raleigh NC), 23 September 1980,
8.

ample you are for those of us who care enough to suffer through these trying times of moral crisis.

Finlator came to realize that many journalists, though secular, were just as concerned about the moral and spiritual ingredient of the public order as he was. Where the church often remained silent about social ills and man's inhumanity to man and where church journals concentrated on denominational housekeeping, Finlator discovered certain highly placed custodians of the press to be very receptive to his social-minded Christianity. One leading publisher, Pete McKnight of the *Charlotte Observer,* shared his feelings with Finlator in a letter dated 4 October 1976: "Although we have lived and worked at a distance I have long felt a kindred interest in the problems of our region and a joint willingness to face them realistically, even when public opinion was running the other way." Naturally such kindred spirits would form a spiritual camaraderie. And in a predominantly Protestant region Finlator became a father-confessor to the worldly, especially with certain newspeople disaffected from organized religion. They saw the church side-stepping the crucial issues of the times or making namby-pamby statements. In Finlator they sensed an authentic voice of the church. In turn, as Finlator encountered the church's refusal to face up to the issues he raised, he relied on these friends in the secular press. He chided the Southern Baptist press for censoring a story that the secular press had picked up and in so doing had actually influenced the denomination to change its stance. (The Baptists of South Africa had stipulated that the Baptists of America could not send a racially integrated evangelistic team to South Africa.) "It is certainly interesting" Finlator wrote, "and even ironic to see how the power of the press affected the Board of a Christian communion. One thinks of Reinhold Niebuhr's observation about how the non-church world can benefit those of the communion of faith if we let it happen."

On another occasion, the editor of a church paper, *Charity and Children,* refused to publish Finlator's endorsement of amnesty for all Vietnam draft evaders, submitted 5 April 1973. Even after

Finlator vigorously protested, the editor ran his letter on 10 June
1973 under the anonymity of "a Raleigh friend."

Instead of the timidity that he so frequently encountered in
the church press, Finlator discovered many men and women in
the secular press who despite their tough-minded and realistic
cynicism had a great appreciation for the concerns of the Gospel
that he promoted. He became their father-confessor.

> Yes, I think I can reveal that many of them use me as as a
> surrogate pastor. So many have given up on the church. And
> many are really moralists and prophets at heart. In that aware-
> ness, I see them as kindred spirits. In many ways their role is
> analogous to mine. They, like the pulpit minister, stand in an ad-
> versarial posture to the publisher, to the advertiser, to the sub-
> scriber. The minister and the journalist have a similar job, vis-
> à-vis these bodies who may be less interested in the truth than
> they are in their own self-interest. Therefore, I have found in
> them, and they seem to have found in me, someone to lean upon.

This mutual attachment commenced at the outset of Finlator's
ministry. The record of his first letter to an editor dates from 16
June 1948, to the *Daily Advance* in Elizabeth City where he was
then pastoring. The Peele family, publishers of the paper, became close friends. Finlator admits to having been born with
printer's ink on his fingers, and he began his literary career early
in life. But it was the common interests of the two professions that
brought them together. "Very early along my way," Finlator recalls,

> I sensed a collegial relationship. We were partners in a common
> cause. We were able to sustain, affirm and promote each other's
> activities. Many of the newspaper people I have known have been
> very fine persons, open to the truth, unhappy with the state of
> things as they are, and dedicated to the commitment to see and
> to publish the truth, and I found that very consonant with what
> I thought should be going on in the pulpit. I sensed that the press
> could be in many ways an extension of the pulpit. I always felt
> that the pulpit is an open thing. It's in the public eye. Nothing
> you can say there can be hidden: it belongs to the public, and
> there's nothing wrong in extending it beyond the borders of the

church. Items that are in the public interest, I have had no hesitation in sharing with the press.

Accordingly, Finlator's cultivation of the press makes a good textbook for ministers. Whenever a critical subject was to be treated in a sermon, he tipped off reporters in advance; afterwards he would dispatch duplicate copies to leading area papers. On key Sundays of the calendar—Bill of Rights Day, Fourth of July, Labor Day, the opening and closing of the State Assembly—he was certain to take a stand to arouse controversy. He addressed numerous letters to editors and reporters congratulating them on their position and their coverage of stories. When a reporter covered any of his own press releases or meetings, he wrote that reporter a personal letter commending him or her just for being present. Above all, Finlator kept members of the press fully informed of his own moves, letting them know in advance when a dramatic turn in an event or gathering might be breaking. The confidentiality and trustworthiness built up over the decades between the two parties paid off for both.

Publishers and editors, coming to respect the quality and the relevance of Finlator's materials, anticipated his releases. Finlator also credits the amount of attention he received to the Southern culture that still maintained a vestige of respect for the village preacher. "It's the South where when a clergyman says something apt on a public issue, he's listened to," he claims. However, it is more likely that he drew attention on account of his flair for controversy and dissent. Finlator's voice sounded above others because so often his was the unpopular voice. He could be counted on to say the unexpected and the unusual. As one observer summarized him, "He had the courage to sing alone." Finlator was quite conscious of expressing the single minority voice. "Offhand I'd say I get more coverage because I am a Baptist, a Southern Baptist, if you please! The press has a habit of looking for a voice within the ranks that sounds a different trumpet."

Few illustrations document this better than Finlator's refusal to endorse Billy Graham in the 1973 Raleigh crusade. The public howled. People were not accustomed to having their popular preacher exposed. Few stands Finlator ever took had such repercussions. Several papers ran his caveat in its entirety; it was carried by the wire services and ultimately reprinted in several national magazines. "Dr. Graham is a phenomenon of our times," Finlator wrote;

> however, his interpretation of the Gospel and mine are not the same. Long ago we took, in Robert Frost's imagery, separate paths and, since I have chosen the one less traveled by, that has made all the difference. Dr. Graham preaches on sin and judgement, as every preacher should, but sins and judgements with him are personal and private, as one theologian puts it, of the Saturday night variety. The Bible also speaks of principalities and powers and spiritual wickedness in the high places. No where do I find Dr. Graham on record as denouncing the sins of corporate powers and economic structures nor of their standing in need of prayer before the doom of God's judgement. His call for law and order is for the man in the street rather than for ITT and his strictures against permissiveness are never directed at the laissez faire practices of economic and industrial giants. I often think of Jesus' remark to the effect that while these things should be done we should not leave undone the weightier matters of the law.
>
> Separation of church and state is a very precious principle to me both as a Baptist and as a civil libertarian. This principle has lost all meaning, however, unless the church can subject the kingdoms of this world under the judgement, as well as the mercy, of Almighty God. Dr. Graham has shown little sympathy for the perennial poor in our society and has regarded their poverty as the result of their unwillingness to participate in their own improvement, not as the result of a system which, while blessing the many, tends to impoverish a large segment of our population. Throughout the struggle for civil rights and racial justice of the 1960's, Dr. Graham remained aloof. When pressed for comment regarding the ravages of war and the inequalities of poverty he refers to some eschatological moment when God in his time and grace shall usher in the era of peace and plenty and justice. . . . I bear no ill will to Dr. Graham and make this statement without hostility or antagonism. But I herewith, as Minister of Pullen Memorial Baptist Church, decline to participate in the crusade.[2]

---

[2]W. W. Finlator, "I'll Skip Billy Graham," *News and Observer* (Raleigh NC), 6 September 1973, 8.

Promptly the *News and Observer,* which had carried the statement in full, bylined on the editorial page, was swamped with angry responses. A couple of weeks later the paper featured a reply by Dr. Graham's daughter, Anne Lotze, who lives in Raleigh and whose husband is Finlator's dentist. Dr. Graham himself addressed a confidential letter to Finlator. The general tenor of the responses may be gathered from one of the published letters.

> I must take exception to the remarks of Mr. Finlator. If Dr. Graham were to follow the desires of this minister, he would have to preach politics, and wild-eyed liberal politics at that. It just so happens that Dr. Graham's beliefs are evidently conservative in nature, but he does not allow his political beliefs to creep into his sermons or writings. No, he preaches sermons that are designed to bring people to Christ, and he leaves their politics to them.

In a personal letter to James Paul on 16 January 1973, Finlator was even more pointed in his criticism of Graham: "The things Billy Graham stands for and preaches can really stand in the way of America coming to confrontation with itself, with its own errors and pride and arrogance and even cruelty both to the people abroad and to the unfortunate at home."

Because Finlator so often stood in the middle of the storm it is a wonder he was not more misrepresented and maligned by the press. On the contrary, he felt that the media treated him fairly, except on those occasions when the WRAL-TV editorials of Jesse Helms, who seemed to have had a personal vendetta against Finlator, attacked him ad hominem. "The press has been extraordinarily kind to me," Finlator says now. "I would have to look hard to find an exception. They have always quoted me, represented me, fairly. Surely there have been times the local press has taken exception to my position, and written editorials taking sharp contrast with me, but they have never attacked me personally."

Nonetheless, Finlator could be cognizant of the damage that media with a vested interest in the status quo could wreak on a prophetic voice. "Many a prophet has been gibbeted in the public press," was a line from his first national article. In Finlator's case, the press seems to have taken pride in its contribution to shaping and amplifying North Carolina's homegrown prophet. Finlator's own files are full of letters in appreciation for this portrait. One admirer wrote on 7 September 1970, "It is so exciting to read your words on the editorial page of the News and Observer. Some countries designate certain artists 'national treasures' and support their work. We think of your voice as one of Raleigh's treasures." Another letter of 9 May 1977 follows the same line. "There are so very few ministers that make the secular news that you can count them on your left thumb, but you are the exception. I always look forward to your news releases in the Charlotte Observer for you have something to say that really counts."

Finlator's cultivation of the press—honoring its integrity, defending its independence, encouraging its prophetic role as the Fourth Estate in democracy, fraternizing with its members—was rewarded with the positive treatment accorded him. Although religion is generally ignored or relegated to the back pages, if not ridiculed outright, Finlator had access to frequent, and oftentimes front page, coverage. Accordingly, his conception of Christianity reached a wider audience than that of the ordinary preacher.

In addition to using the press as his extended ministry, Finlator turned to labor and the union halls. Only two or three other causes elicited such strong and sustained loyalty. Labor repaid his devotion by welcoming him personally into all its deliberations, even when he gave critical support, and by making him officially the chaplain of the North Carolina AFL-CIO. In the year of his retirement that organization awarded him a plaque reading, "A Preacher Who Practices What He Preaches." What this action says about the nature of labor unions in the one state in America where workers are least organized is significant. What it says about a prominent Southern Baptist preacher is even more revealing. Finlator was indisputably and unapologetically a friend of unions.

There are two sources for Finlator's commitment. One was his father's membership in the railroad union. The other was his devotion to Jesus whom he regarded as both a worker and a friend of working people. He felt that the church, particularly the church in the South, had betrayed Jesus in its failure to endorse labor and had been silent in the face of the exploitation of laborers accompanying the industrialization of the South. At the very time when the region's birthrate produced the nation's largest supply of cheap labor once the flood of immigration subsided, and when its commercial bosses attracted industry with their blatant advertisements guaranteeing a pool of nonunion workers, the Southern Protestant churches, though drawing heavily upon working-class membership, shut their eyes to the distress of the workers. Cheap labor, bad working conditions, unfair profits, lack of industrial democracy, all were no concern of theirs. Christianity had nothing to say in the marketplace: Christ saves souls, not jobs. Their negativism toward unions might be theological, but the same preachers were not reluctant to preach the virtues of the work ethic and the divinity of the free market system.

Against this backdrop, Finlator is indeed a peculiarity on the Southern scene. No wonder he was honored by the labor unions and suspected by the churches. Yet his placement in his ministry of five decades—three of his four pastorates were "First" churches—belies his defiance of accepted tradition. "First" churches, county-seat churches, are the kingpins of the status quo. Even in his fourth and longest pastorate, the Pullen Memorial Church, there was little sympathy for blue-collar workers. In spite of Pullen's free pulpit, he was obliged to confess in the end that his stand on labor "became one of the chief causes of unhappiness with some members."

At the very moment he was the preacher of a middle-class, white-collar, sophisticated campus church, he had become the chaplain of the state labor union and the platform preacher on the Southern labor scene. His second pulpit was the union hall. His larger congregation included the people on the picket lines he joined, the union members in their conventions and at their banquets where he gave the invocations and preached. Labor journals published his messages. Labor leaders became his close friends. "I am unabashedly a friend of labor and industrial unionism," Finlator says.

My father was a railroad conductor and a member of the Order of Railroad Conductors, a labor union which gave dignity and security to his work. He kept all three of us children in college in the heart of the depression. Whatever gain in working conditions, wages and hours and health and retirement have come to the laboring people of America have come through their unions. It is just that, pure and simple. I have been privileged to stand with labor leaders in support of minimum wages and in opposition to the unjust and the unsporting right-to-work laws. I have strongly endorsed labor's committee on political education and have encouraged the unions to a policy of bringing our black citizens into full membership. I have urged the extension of labor's concern to migrant and unorganized farm workers, who of all groups stand most in need of labor's friendship. I proudly stood with the AFL-CIO in its dramatization of grievances against the Carolina Power and Light Company. And I have gladly contributed my bit towards exploring areas where church and labor might work more closely together in common causes. It has been difficult for me as a child of labor to see why collective strength as represented in, say, the Merchants Association, the Chamber of Commerce, the National Association of Manufacturers, the Farm Bureau, medical, bar, real estate and bankers associations, could suddenly become a thing of fear and dread, to be legislated against and harried out of the land, when the working class seeks similar refuge and security. I always felt that what was good for Paul and Silas, and for the Hebrew children, was good enough for me.

During the very years when the churches of the South were mostly opposed to unionism, a history thoroughly documented in Liston Pope's *Millhands and Preachers,* and in its forty-year followup, *Spindles and Spires,* Finlator was devoting his energies to bringing the churches and the unions together. He gained for himself the title, "dean of those few preachers who side with labor." He became vice-president of Southerners for Economic Justice at its opening conference held at Lake Junaluska in November 1977. "The churches are lined up emotionally and instinctively with management," Finlator told that assembly. "Our institutions get their focus from management-oriented people and our official boards are made up of management people, people from the chambers of commerce, the banks, the merchants bureaus. But if you read the Bible carefully, you'll find out that the

Bible through the prophets—Amos, Isaiah, Jesus—has always identified God as oriented toward the poor, the dispossessed and the exploited. The church today is just at the opposite side. I see our task as bringing the church in line with the Gospel."

Finlator labored tirelessly to bring the two groups together. He described one such meeting about the J. P. Stevens boycott, held at Roanoke Rapids in September 1980.

> We gathered in the Union Hall and then went to a delicious steak dinner. Afterwards we sat around the tables and talked about what we were to do and what the situation was at present. We came to know each other better. There were some twenty of us from the Methodists and the United Church and the Baptists and Catholics; there may have been others also. We divided up afterwards and went to see a special home where a retiree from the mill was living and talked about the parsimonious pensions, if any, and the attitude of the workers. We each then went and stood on the lines outside the large mills and subsequently gathered in the Hall to hammer out the statement which we will release to the press. We also agreed to send a delegation to Ray Marshall of the Department of Labor in Washington. Furthermore we plan to send our statement to the religious community. Following this 15 or 20 of the Union leaders came in after the four o'clock shift and we listened to them and talked with them. Quite a meeting indeed and all of us felt mutually strengthened.

Appropriately, his first editorial as an "official" journalist had been devoted to the same theme. In "The Southern Baptists and the Labor Management Crisis," Finlator charged, "If the minister fails to apply the principles of the Gospel to the labor crisis, he denies the relevancy of Christianity to the corporate attitudes and actions of men. To rightly divide the word of truth is to preach the whole gospel and the whole gospel has a message for the issues in this controversy."[3] Within six months he targeted the subject again: "The important thing for the churches to remember at the outset is . . . that the labor movement as a whole has struggled and progressed without benefit of clergy and church,

---

[3]Finlator, "The Southern Baptists and the Labor Management Crisis," *Christian Frontiers* 1 (January 1946): 32.

conscious for the most part of a silent if not overt opposition of institutional religion."[4]

Thirty-five years later, in an article called "Economic Justice
and the Religious Community," Finlator felt obliged to repeat the
charge. "If the witness of the mainline churches in these areas has
been one largely of silence and impotence, the rise in power of the
fundamentalist faiths pushes religious witness to a kind of aggressive unconcern." This claim is preceded by a battery of questions.

> Where is the church today when measures are proposed to
> amend these heaped-up, raw injustices of the years? What has the
> church to say now about brown-lung and black-lung diseases? I'm
> listening hard. What word does it have for affirmative action
> quotas and ratios and for numerical remedies used in leveling in-
> justice within employment? What word about increasing concen-
> tration of minorities in urban ghettos? How does it deal with built-
> in and manipulated unemployment? What protest does it have
> for the migrant farm workers, "the wretched of the earth" who
> live and move and have their limited being almost completely
> bereft of every basic protection of the Bill of Rights which we take
> for granted for ourselves? What about the aging and medically
> indigent who are not getting the medicine and care they need and
> who are too proud to ask for help? Somewhere Martin Luther
> wrote about the "wicked silence" of Christians.[5]

During that long span (1946-1981), Finlator's reputation as a
minister with a staunch allegiance to labor was firmly forged. He
was ever present at their annual conventions and on their picket
lines and for their organizational rallies. His prayers and words
of encouragement became sentiments treasured by labor. His
personal friends included their leaders such as Boyd Payton, Mil-
lard Barbee, and Wilbur Hobby. Within his own church, his annual Labor Day sermons became celebrated pieces, widely
published in the region and nation. He often went before the leg-

---

[4]Finlator, "Christianity in Spite of the Churches," *Christian Frontiers* 2
(February 1947): 179.

[5]Finlator, "Economic Justice and the Religious Community," *Fair Measure*
4 (March 1981): 2.

islature and congressional committees to plead against unfair laws about to be enacted against labor. His first public appointment was to the Governor's Committee on Migrant Labor, in the late 1940s. Thirty years later, as chairman of the North Carolina Advisory Committee to the U.S. Civil Rights Commission, he headed an investigation of migrant labor conditions that was issued as a study-book, "Where Mules Outrate Men," in May 1979.

Finlator came to feel perfectly at home within the labor movement, enjoying the company of labor activists and endearing himself to them. They credit him with influencing labor to embrace wider human concerns. "As I look back," Finlator says now,

> I am somewhat surprised that they accepted me as well as they did. My reputation for exposing racism, my identification with civil liberties, my stand against the war, and my pressing for unions to be concerned about all workers, not just the crafts, all of these matters came up for discussion in union meetings. They were taking a great risk in bringing me in, and I must pause to give appreciation to certain of their leaders who braved that risk to defend me. I was even able to challenge the president of the national AFL-CIO, George Meany, for not dissociating himself and the working people of America from the Vietnam war. I can honestly say that the leadership I have worked with, on picket lines, in strike rallies, at all the conventions, have been among the finest people I have known. I don't know just how I "got in" with the unions except for a natural interest and desire to support them. Across the years they have included me and made me one of "the brethren." As a matter of fact I have run into numerous labor leaders who were active Christians and very church conscious. They have told me privately that they wished their own ministers might be active in the union but they seemed to hold no grudge against their ministers for their nonparticipation. They seemed to understand the predicament of a Southern preacher with regard to the power structure which so often muzzles the pulpit.

Although he endeared himself to union people, his behavior did little to "win friends and influence people" among that large segment of the population that viewed unions with suspicion, evaluating them in the light of the vices of big labor with its violence, its underworld connections, and its greed and ostentation. They thought Finlator had sullied the pulpit and overstepped the bounds of clergy concern. He had, they said, "sold out" the gospel in his partisanship. Over the decades his mail was laced with such criticism. Of the hundreds of letters of this nature, two will be cited, both from the later years of his ministry. The first is a letter from the president of a textile company on 7 September 1977; the second is Finlator's own letter in reply to a Baptist pastor who had attacked him for aligning with the unions in their use of violence, dated 13 December 1979.

> I am certainly not impressed with your stand and your actions concerning the problems that J. P. Stevens Company is having with the Amalgamated Clothing and Textile Workers Union. I worked for J. P. Stevens from 1950 to 1961 and frankly, I can truthfully say that I have never worked for a corporation that is any more fair to their employees than they were. It is my opinion and I am certainly more qualified to have an opinion than all the Baptist ministers and all the Catholic priests in the United States, that you are dead wrong in the stand you are taking against J. P. Stevens.

> There is no doubt about the fact that violence does exist in the union, violence against employers and violence within the union themselves, against each other! No one could read the record of labor movement in North Carolina and close his eyes to this fact. There is violence on the other side. All of us have heard of the goon squads and professional strike breakers. We also know about bringing in the National Guard, the crackdown by police busts, etc., almost always on the side of management. The answer of course is that we are against violence, period, and it's the duty of the government to take a neutral stand, act as umpire, and hold violence from whatever source to an absolute minimum.

Finlator's sympathies were with labor from the beginning of his ministry. The real question pertains to the moment he first threw himself into the nitty-gritty of the union struggle, proving himself different from other preachers by being willing to bear the scars of the battle alongside the working person. His theoretical identity was well known; he had publicized the plight of the migrant laborers and had sided with the striking lumberyard workers when he lived at Elizabeth City. But it was not until the bloody and prolonged textile workers' strike at Henderson in 1959 that he was baptized by fire. He entered that fray quite unexpectedly, perhaps in the least likely way. The local association of Baptist churches dared invite him as an outsider on 21 October, specifically to address them on the four crucial questions for Christian living, which they designated as alcoholism, church-state separation, race relations and labor-management conflict. True to form, Finlator rang the changes on each, stirring plenty of controversy, but due to the intensity of the feelings about the local strike, what he said about labor drew the most attention.

> The church and its leaders dare not look the other way when in the dynamic of industrial strife clear ethical issues are at stake.
>
> It may come with ill grace for an afternoon visitor to take to task his fellow churchmen in a community that has suffered what only the residents of Henderson can really know. An outsider, safe from the awful realities, can be presumptuous and for this I beg forgiveness. Yet as outsiders we wondered again and again if the local churches had no word at all to speak when the entire community was in the throes of an agonizing struggle.
>
> That the church spoke the quiet word of solace and strength to her people, I doubt not, and this is always important, as is also the office of the church to condemn violence. But with men out of work week after week, with the honest expectation of their jobs crumbling into dust at the last hour, with the fear in their faces and the despair in their hearts that will drive any man to extremities, with a state government which in the final analysis had nothing more to offer than the Highway Patrol and the National Guard, and with a respected union deliberately "busted," the church, so far as I know, never said a mumbling word! Surely, my brethren, this is what Martin Luther would again call "wicked silence," and we confess with shame that we, too, on the outside have participated in this silence.
>
> The church does have a word for management-labor relations and that word is human dignity and human value which must always be placed before all other considerations.

Overnight Finlator found himself in the middle of the dispute. His speech was printed in major state papers. Labor leaders wel-

comed him as their new champion. Wives of unemployed workers, who as mothers were struggling to feed and clothe their
families as the months dragged on in this strife-torn town,
scratched notes of gratitude for coming to their aid. Workers expressed to him their disappointment in the failure of their local
churches to provide intervention and relief for their physical
needs. Governor Luther Hodges took the stand to rebut Finlator's
criticism of the administration's role. One clergyman wrote to rationalize the noninvolvement of Henderson's clergy. Seldom has
a preacher's sermon in a minor ecclesiastical assembly in an ob-
scure town aroused so much public furor.

The very next morning, Boyd Payton, state president of the
AFL-CIO, addressed Finlator in a letter: "This morning's paper
with the story about your speech gave me a lift like I haven't had
for months. Thank you very much." He invited Finlator to speak
once more in Henderson, this time on 14 November, to mark the
anniversary of the first full year of the strike. Handwritten letters came from several citizens of the town. Two were written by
women.

> Please accept my gratitude for the stand you have take [sic]
> in the strike situation in our town. I'm glad some ministers have
> enough backbone to express their convictions. We have a pray-
> ing people here and God has been so good and we feel we are in
> the right. Also we think others feel the same way but just want
> to be on the company's side for the love of money. We are hard
> working people—all we ask for is a meager living. I'm glad that
> the Lord never left us nor forsakes us. And my trust is in Him.

> Thank you for speaking about our strike situation. It was true
> what you said the Governor calmly sitting down and giving us no
> assistance. For we went to see Mr. Hodges and pleaded for him
> to come to us. Still we have received no help from our state and
> local agents. We even appealed to Washington to Senator [sic]
> Cooley and others with what results? All we received was a batch
> of state patrolmen. We have Christian people who are praying for
> both union and for a peaceful settlement.

Another letter, this one from the Sunday School superintendent of a Baptist Church in Henderson, referred to the local church response.

> I want to congratulate you on your statements made at the First Church concerning the strike situation here in Henderson. I think that you are 100% correct in that the pastors, excepting two, did not say a word in behalf of the people in this crisis. A few ministers—not Baptists—did what little they could do for the people but I am sorry to say they were pastors who do not carry weight with the leaders of this fair city. I am neither a striker nor an agitator and this is the first time I have expressed myself to anyone outside of my community. I am proud of a man of your ability and position that has the courage to make such statements. As everyone knows and a lot of people are learning North Carolina is fast becoming recognized as "Hodges' Slave Labor State." This strike has put our community back twenty years spiritually. This is and has been my deepest concern. May many more ministers and leaders of religious groups start remembering the right of the working man.

Many letter writers, especially some leaders of industry, expressed dissatisfaction with Finlator's intervention. One letter from an engineering company president displays their mood.

> If your knowledge of facts of the Bible is as inaccurate and biased as your statements relative to the Henderson strike, Lord help your congregation.
> The State of North Carolina has enacted laws which prohibit violence and destruction of property and there is no law which prohibits peaceful picketing. Your statements would appeal to the emotional, immature and unbalanced personality which—thank God—is not the majority of North Carolina.
> I have utmost confidence in the leadership of the state and needless to say our prestige ranks high in all the states that I visit.

Other letter writers expressed disgust at a preacher "meddling" in the business of labor-management relations rather than "preaching the gospel." This one is typical.

> See in today's News and Observer that you criticized local pastors in Henderson for failure to inject themselves into the Harriet-Henderson strike of union employees. It occurs to me you

won't attempting to preach the Gospel as you are supposed to do, rather than trying to further augment and stir up strife and hatred. The very idea of your going to Henderson and taking upon yourself the assignment and authority to upbraid the ministers about a local matter that does not concern you and that you know nothing about, is facetious and shows a lack of commonsense.

Forced to the forefront by the publicity, Finlator could hardly remain on the sidelines thereafter. He was asked by labor leaders to visit strike-torn towns to bring moral support, to intervene where possible with the management and the city leaders who were usually in line with company policy, and to comfort the families of strikers. In the extended garbage workers case in Raleigh, which dragged on through most of the 1960s, he pled for them before the mayor and the city council and marched with them in the picket lines. He joined in the protest against Carolina Power and Light Company when it contracted with an antiunion construction firm in 1969. He was constantly before the legislature pleading against unfair labor laws. He vehemently opposed the newly introduced "right-to-work" bill, and led a regional campaign in 1961-62 against its enactment, although he was unsuccessful. Marion Wright, a prominent Southern lawyer who was then president of the Southern Regional Council, wrote on 2 April 1962,

> I would applaud this evidence that at least one spokesman for the Baptist Church in the South feels that he has a duty to express himself on social issues. . . . So far as I am aware, your statement is the first expression from a responsible Baptist voice on economic matters. I hope others may emulate your example.

However, Finlator's efforts to secure from his own denomination endorsement for labor's goals were largely unsuccessful. His voice in labor's behalf naturally gained the best platform within labor organizations. In 1960 the union published his address, "Conscience in the South," and he delivered his first speech before a labor convention on 27 March 1960, which was printed in full by the *News and Observer* under the title "What's Right, What's Wrong in North Carolina." In 1962 he addressed the International Typographical Union on "The Rights and Responsibilities of Labor." Subsequently, in the succeeding years he was a featured speaker at the annual state labor conventions and rarely did he allow the opportunity to pass without a major pronouncement. His speech on 20 September 1965, "A New Look at Labor," garnered considerable reaction. Earlier that month, the *Charlotte Observer* published his Labor Day sermon, "The Church and Big Business." In 1969 his public letter challenging President Meany's endorsement of the Vietnam war made national headlines.

A sampling of his activities in the 1970s includes, besides the usual convention appearances, marching with sanitation workers in Raleigh (1970), identifying with the United Farm Workers (1971), participating in the Hobby Rally, a coalition of minor political units in that campaign year (1972), a plug for unions in the *Charlotte Observer* (1973), a Labor Day rally in Charlotte (1974), appearances in the J. P. Stevens unionization at Roanoke and Wallace (1975), a widely circulated speech, "Economic Liberty" (1976), a petition to the Committee on Education and Labor of the U.S. House and an organizer of Southerners for Economic Justice (1977), his notorious "stockholder" speech to the stockholders of Stevens (1978), his exposure of antilabor ploys (1979), and his article in a national journal, "Unsporting to Labor" (1980). Two of these actions drew nationwide attention—his support of the growing boycott of Stevens goods because of the corporation's backward labor practices, and his share in removing the Institute of Labor Policy from the campus of his alma mater.

Finlator had given himself freely to labor's crusade designed to force the J. P. Steven's Company to unionize. Since it had dozens of plants across the South, to break the company would affect many communities. As a ploy, his labor friends set him up so that he could "invade" the Stevens annual stockholders meeting, 1979. They conceived the idea of buying some stock and letting Finlator infiltrate the cavernous Textile Hall at Stevens headquarters in Greenville, South Carolina. Now a bona fide stockholder, Finlator somehow gained the floor in the presence of 4,000 other stockholders. "My name is Finlator," he announced.

> I am a Baptist preacher from Raleigh, North Carolina. Mr. Chairman, I wish you would pay your workers more money. And

I have a selfish reason for this request. You see, Mr. Finley, I suspect that most of your 40,000 workers are Southern Baptists. I'm also a Southern Baptist—a Baptist minister who is approaching retirement. If your workers had more money, they would give more to their Baptist churches. The churches would in kind give more to the Southern Baptist Convention, which would increase the retirement benefits for its ministers. So you see, Mr. Chairman, I have a selfish reason for wanting you to treat your workers better.

Chairman James Finley and other stockholders were grandly amused, and Finlator had his audience right where he wanted them, as well as the press and others who might otherwise have ignored the position of a prounion stockholder.

The year before, in a letter dated 3 April 1978, he had called his own alma mater to task for sheltering an institute within its Law School that purported to devise antiunion tactics for use by corporations.

The Wake Forest Institute of Labor Policy Analysis is, in my judgement, not a bona fide structure for an open and objective study of labor and labor-management relations. On the contrary, it seems little more than a front for anti-labor indoctrination enjoying the respectability of being associated with a university. It is funded independently from sources of an anti-labor orientation and therefore has no more place on a university campus than a similar institute set up and supported by the AFL-CIO.

A positive response from the University to his challenge and its move to reject any restraints upon its academic freedom, even those imposed by its controlling agency, the Baptist denomination, earned for Wake Forest the Alexander Meiklejohn Award for Academic Freedom. Finlator's letter to the awarding committee, citing the University's courage in ridding itself of the Institute, was a factor in the decision to make the award.

On 26 August 1979, Finlator sent a message to the textile workers of Roanoke Rapids congratulating them on the fifth anniversary of the establishment of their union.

In your long struggle and cause you have placed all true lovers of freedom in your debt. . . . Please therefore never feel that you are alone. Roanoke Rapids is everywhere. Heaven knows that we have not come to your side with the courage and commitment you have every right to expect of us. But you must not feel deserted. The NLRB has vindicated you time and time again. The federal courts have consistently ruled in your favor and will continue to do so. Church leadership has expressed its moral conscience for you. The boycott represents rank and file support. All of us share in your celebration today and assure you of our support in the long, long way you still have to go before we reach these sunlit uplands.

Despite all the encouragement he meted out to others, Finlator himself was painfully aware that in actual fact the union movement was losing ground. Taking time for a personal word before he gave the invocation at the state labor convention in Raleigh, 16 September 1981, he shared his distress.

American organized labor has fallen on hard, hard times. The ranks are decimated, the spirit is crushed, the singing is gone. Everywhere dismay and disarray—labor is against the ropes and they are moving in for the kill.

Out there, they are asking for more right-to-work enforcement; they are asking for more decertifications of unions and more antilabor, repressive legislation; they are asking for more concessions in wages and working conditions and more no-strike pledges; they are asking for more flight of industry from long established union areas to the nonunionized and cheap labor areas of the South.

I point out these bleak and dismal truths for one reason: we must learn the importance of the big word we hear so much about from Poland—SOLIDARITY.

Finlator's constant words of encouragement for labor were greatly appreciated by its leaders. E. A. Britt, the latest of his Christian friends who had become president of the state AFL-CIO, wrote to him on 30 September 1982.

Thank you very much for being with us for the 25th Annual Convention. Your inspiring invocation and your comments to the delegates were very much appreciated. We are very much honored to have you as the official chaplain of our state organization.

A similar letter issued from the International Union of Operating Engineers on 18 May 1983.

> We were all stirred by your talk on labor leadership and religion. I have gone back to the themes you raised many times since Saturday. I'm sure others have done the same.

Finlator conceived of his presence in organized labor as an extension of his Christian ministry. Besides providing pastoral care, he could act the prophet and the critic. This fact was not lost on labor. His union friends could be as apprehensive about his pronouncements as his church friends. Bill Mixon, president of Local 54 (Raleigh) of the International Typographical Union, wrote to him on 7 May 1962, following his speech to the union.

> I couldn't help being amused with the almost certain knowledge that most of us present during your speech were on the edge of our chair, anticipating—and wondering—what next might come forth from "this mountain called Finlator." What did come forth was blessed inspiration endowed only by God. . . . Your speech was very significant in that you gave local unions (in this area) what I think is the first *direct* prod toward true brotherhood.

In that speech Finlator had chided labor for excluding blacks and supporting a militaristic economy. He had urged the union to back the migrant workers, the rewriting of tax laws in favor of the poor, the development of a total-coverage medical plan for every citizen, and a host of other social programs. The national president of ITU, Elmer Brown of Colorado Springs, learning of his Raleigh speech, addressed him on 2 May 1962.

> On behalf of the 114,000 members of I.T.U. and indeed, of all union men and women everywhere, I would like to offer you our heartfelt commendations for your outstanding courage and perseverance in advocating the Christian precepts of the organized labor movement in America, and in appreciation for the far-reaching encouragement you have given our worthy cause. We in the labor movement, and the entire American working force, are indebted to you for your efforts to preserve the concepts of human dignity in these days when man's inhumanity to his fellow

man appears to be on the increase. We cannot long survive without the spiritual and moral encouragement of men like yourself.

Finlator's rapport with laboring people, particularly with those in the South, strengthened over the years. Southern labor activists were conscious of being an unwanted minority; they understood what tremendous odds they were up against trying to organize; they realized their struggle was running a generation behind the rest of the nation. The irony of their predicament was that at the very moment many laborers in other parts of the nation were becoming disillusioned with unions—bosses living it up, bureaucracy consuming the excessive dues, and corruption in some big unions—they were whipping up enthusiasm for solidarity. Their affection for Finlator derived not merely from their appreciation of him as one prominent civic leader who dared take their side but from their basic respect for God and the church. Southern labor had not become alienated from the church to the extent that labor had in the rest of the nation; it still retained its evangelical, pietistic and biblical connections. Finlator became "our preacher"; he symbolized for them what they expected from a God who cares.

Finlator did not let them down. While his alignment with labor tended to be less critical than any other of his ideological commitments—almost to the point of "labor right or wrong"—he viewed his stance as one avenue for his larger compassion for all misused and neglected peoples. In his Labor Day sermon of 6 September 1965, he declared,

> The church must take a new look at labor by taking a new look at the New Testament. As a child of God, man, any man, "even the least of these my brethren" is by virtue of his humanity of infinite worth regardless of productive capacity. The lost, the despised, the diseased, the handicapped, the forgotten, in short, the disadvantaged, were the people sought out by Jesus for no other reason than that they were there and God loved them. Hence the parables of the Lost Coin, the Lost Sheep, and the Lost Son.

He used the same biblical language when addressing union audiences. Typical of this approach are these lines from his 1977 invocation at the state convention.

Teach us to realize that our hope and salvation lie not in self
seeking but in our commitment to the common good, and, that
where any is deprived all are deprived, where any suffer injustice all must face the consequences, where any is not liberated all
are unfree. Forbid that we make haste to become rich at the expense of our neighbor, whether near or far, and deliver us all,
whether rich or poor, from envy and covetousness. Let none of us
shun the rightful claim of our sister and brother upon our time
and energy and good in the spirit and mandate that from those
to whom much has been given much will be required.

Such language was not lost on common working people. For instance, responding to the press account of the Labor Day sermon
cited above, the Catawba Central Labor Union of Rock Hill, South
Carolina, composed of nine locals, had its secretary Jack Porter
write to Finlator on 14 September 1965. "At our meeting Monday
night, the delegates were read clippings out of the Charlotte Observer of your views about labor and what should be done to back
labor. The delegates voted to send you a letter commending you
on your stand."

Labor unions never doubted that this preacher stood by their
side, and as his years of loyal presence expanded they let him
know of their affection. Typical are two letters, both from union
officials—namely, Scott Hoyman in a letter of 16 October 1974,
and Harold McIver, on 3 September 1974.

I want to thank you very much on behalf of the Textile Workers Union for your wonderful contribution to our conference in
Charlotte on Sunday afternoon. The effect of the message which
you gave on those in attendance was not duplicated by any other
speaker.

I want to express thanks for your contribution to the success
of the Roanoke Rapids campaign. Your message to our pre-elec-
tion rally gave inspiration to the assembled Steven's workers and
to our staff. Hopefully, it will open the door to a new, progressive
south. You can be proud of the part you have played in opening
that door.

Such letters were Finlator's sole reward as he exhausted himself traveling the countryside in behalf of labor. There was no

payment for these services. Moreover he had to sandwich these engagements into his already heavy schedule as a loyal pastor and a civic leader with other pressing duties. He gathered friends among laboring people and found satisfaction in having a wider audience for what he took to be his God-given mission. To Scott Hoyman he replied on 21 October 1974, "I send you this brief word to thank you genuinely and warmly for the honor of being with you and the other distinguishing labor leaders at the important rally last Sunday. . . I am always honored to be identified with you and the cause of labor."

What made Finlator so indispensable to labor in the South was that he could in no wise be labeled "an outsider." The standard charge against unionization efforts in the region was that they originated with outsiders paid to disturb "the good old ways." The memory of carpetbaggers who had come from the North to exploit a helpless South was still vivid, and this animosity was reinforced currently by the obvious evidence that the national labor leaders plotted to unionize the South, that their organizers frequently had Northern bases, and that money to sustain Southern strikers had to be raised outside the South. Finlator, on the contrary, defied all these accusations. He was as Southern as one could be, a hometown boy in a Southern Baptist pulpit. No one could accuse him of being an outside meddler, a fly-by-night agent, a liberal being paid for his tears, or someone having a lark slumming. Finlator was on the scene, late and soon, invariably defending his stance by claiming he was only doing what was best for the South and by daring his detractors to deny that he was really the South at its best. Very early in his career certain astute observers had caught the significance of this fact. Twice media profiles honored him for this contribution, once when he was named "Tar Heel of the Week" in the Raleigh *News and Observer* on 8 November 1953, and again in the *Raleigh Magazine,* in the Fall of 1969. "The church ought to be on the side of the people," Finlator told the *Raleigh Magazine.* "I mean the people who can't protect themselves, the poor, the ignorant, the black, the hungry, the houseless and the badly housed. That accounts for some of the things I do. I believe that means unionism for the poor people, racial justice for the black man, an end to the cold war economy that is working against the poor."[6]

Finlator's championship of unions and of laboring people cost him loss of influence within the power structure of the church and the state and caused some unrest within his own congregation. Some members of his church thought he harped too often and too loud on the subject. The irony is that when he himself was under pressure to resign from the Pullen pulpit the protection he had trumpeted so long as a major benefit of union membership was lacking for him. Long before, when he had no inkling of such a dilemma, he jokingly acknowledged, "Unfortunately this does not apply to 'hard-shelled' Baptists who let every preacher look out for himself." The larger, civic community was even less friendly. As has been seen, they let him know of their disapproval and for the most part they closed their portals to him. He was keenly conscious of this deprivation.

> My "outspoken stance" has of course caused me to lose opportunities to speak in the chambers of commerce and the civic clubs. This is a price one must be willing and even happy to pay—though to tell the truth the people I grew up with and went to school with and graduated with are nearly all in this part of the ball park. Nonetheless I am willing to continue saying, "There is no real hope for Southerners without good reputable labor unions. There is no way to bring about justice and equity and fair distribution of the good things of our economy without strong unionism." And even as poorly organized as are Southern laborers, the very existence of unions, their threat of growth, improves the behavior of business and corporate executives. Moreover, anyone who professes concern and interest in poor people and depressed people has to confront realistically the problem of unions.

During these years, 1935-1985, the Christian communion to which Finlator belonged went on its merry way, building a mighty bureaucratic machine, collecting vast amounts of money, and, in the process, becoming the largest Protestant denomination in America. It took not the slightest note that it had produced a

---

[6]Joe Doster, "Raleigh Personality," *Raleigh Magazine* 1 (Fall 1969): 10.

preacher who had become a celebrated friend of labor. Only in his retirement, when he was in his seventies, did a single agency of the denomination tip its hat to his achievement. Southern Baptist Seminary's magazine, *Review and Expositor,* devoted its Spring 1984 issue to "Christianity and Economic Responsibility" and requested him to contribute an article. In response, he wrote,

> Economic justice will not be addressed by the church unless the minister is willing to become involved in the arena. . . . And so I have not hesitated to join what today are called the secular humanists (a term that does not scare me) simply because demons were being cast out and miracles of justice performed in some other name than the church—especially since the church so often opts out. I have remembered that Jesus made friends with all sorts and conditions of people. I urge all ministers who yearn for economic justice and decency to remember labor unions when they think of low wages and poor working conditions.[7]

In one short paragraph, Finlator had shared with his readers his formula for cultivating the press and boosting labor.

---

[7]Finlator, "The Ministry and Economic Justice," *Review and Expositor* 81 (Spring 1984): 247.

Chapter Four

FIGHTING RACISM

MARTIN LUTHER KING, JR. wrote in his famous "Letter from the Birmingham Jail" that our generation would have to repent "not merely for the vitriolic words and actions of the bad people, but for the appalling silence of the good people." He continued to register his deep disappointment with the leadership of the white churches, whom he had thought might be natural allies in the freedom movement but who turned out to be "more cautious than courageous and [who] have remained silent behind the anesthetizing security of stained glass windows." Not a single white minister met Dr. King's expectations of going with him all the way in what he considered the Christian way in race relations.

A leading voice in the chorus of social transition belongs to the white liberal, whether he speak through the government, the church, the voluntary welfare agencies or the civil rights movement. Over the last few years many Negroes have felt that their most troublesome adversary was not the obvious bigot of the Ku

Klux Klan or the John Birch Society, but the white liberal who
is more devoted to "order" than to justice, who prefers tranquil-
ity to equality.

The "Christian way" for Dr. King meant the tactics of challenging segregation head-on—by direct action, by creative nonviolence, by deliberately breaking immoral laws. When King's
freedom movement began in 1955, few ministers in either the
North or South appreciated his method. Finlator himself was still
resorting to the customary liberal stance of treating the Negro
with respect, an etiquette of personal relations within the frame-
work of separate but equal. The catchwords were "brotherhood,"
"fellowship," and "interracial" progress. Certainly few white religious leaders in the South imagined complete integration.

Thirty years prior to Dr. King's Birmingham Letter, Finlator,
while enrolled in seminary, had been moved by the desires of a
young black wanting to be trained for the ministry but shut out
by the seminary so that he tutored him in his own dormitory room.
One of his upperclass friends, Clarence Jordan, was stirring the
waters of traditionalism by devoting himself full time to this
"missionary calling" on the local scene in the city of Louisville,
Kentucky, but few were willing to follow him. When Finlator returned to Eastern North Carolina to undertake his profession,
first in a circuit of three churches centering in Pittsboro, he was
soon voicing his uneasiness about the traditional approach. By the
time he became pastor of the First Baptist Church in Elizabeth
City, his peers were saying that he was known to preach mostly
on three subjects: sex, labor, and race. His earliest published misgivings about racial discrimination appeared in the *Biblical Recorder,* on 1 April 1942; commenting on the war against the Nazis,
he asked whether America might be practicing Hitler's racism
here at home. He returned to the theme in the same journal on 17
June. By 15 March 1944, he dared devote a full article to the matter, entitled "Pastors and Prejudice." He appealed to the pulpit to
take the lead in abolishing racism rather than leaving it to "so-
ciologists and secular reformers." "Yet I do despair," he wrote, "to
learn how entrenched it is in the pulpit . . . I do not mean to sit in

judgement upon my brethren (heaven knows my own heart is not right yet on this race score)."[1]

By the time Finlator began writing editorials for *Christian Frontiers,* in 1946, his enlightenment on the problem of racism had been radically altered by the Myrdal study of 1944, *An American Dilemma,* and by President Truman's Civil Rights Commission report of 1947, *To Secure These Rights.* He urged Southern churches not to ignore these pivotal studies. Already he was aligning himself with pioneer movements for racial justice in the South, the Fellowship of Southern Churchmen and the Southern Conference Educational Fund, both begun in the 1930s. Ministers in Dixieland rarely raised the colors with such groups. Certain crucial personal encounters also opened his eyes to the necessity of moving beyond the stage of granting common courtesies within the bounds of racism. Once, while on vacation at the beach, Finlator and his wife watched while a white soldier and his nonwhite wife were denied service at a restaurant. Finlator leaped from his table and followed the offended couple in order to apologize for their mistreatment. He urged them to return with him while he negotiated their rights with the management. They rejected his offer, but he returned to upbraid the manager and in turn to refuse to eat in the restaurant himself.

However, other than personalizing the racial indignities he happened to observe and pressing for justice and kindness within the segregated system, he had not arrived at the social freedom of "a desegregated church within a desegregated society." Not until 1946 did the Federal Council of Churches in the United States take this position, a stance that provoked many Southern church leaders to dissatisfaction with the Council. Finlator was not to utter that slogan in a public address until 1959. It should be noted that the Protestant church throughout the world did not reach that position much more quickly. When the first World Council of Churches gathered in Amsterdam in 1948 there was only a passing mention of racism. Not until its second gathering, at Evanston in 1954, and then only under the prodding of the dis-

---

[1]W. W. Finlator, "Pastors and Prejudice," *Biblical Recorder* 110 (15 March 1944): 7.

tinguished Southern black educator and preacher, Dr. Benjamin
Mays, did they issue a report on "The Church Amid Racial Tensions." It admitted that "the majority of [Protestant] churches acknowledge that the Gospel requires equality among races, and an
end to discrimination, injustice and segregation." It confessed that
"they all too frequently, in official policy as well as in practice,
put forward a policy of gradual attainment of these goals, turning deliberately away from the absolute requirements of the Gospel at this point." Finlator attended this assembly at Evanston,
though not as a delegate, because Southern Baptists had elected
not to cooperate. Besides, Southern Baptists at this time were nowhere near this stage of commitment to abandoning racism.

But for this Southern Baptist from Eastern North Carolina,
the race issue became his most crucial concern. Throughout his
career it would implicate him in more controversy than any of his
social activism and shroud his retirement from the pastorate in
misunderstanding and bitterness. He did not choose to make it
the primary issue of his life, but within Southern culture he found
that racism was inextricably mixed with everything else. What
marks Finlator is that he seemed more ready to face the intricacy
of the problem. He did not back away from it as so many of his
fellow ministers found it convenient to do. Thoroughly baptized
in the Southern mythos himself, he nonetheless appreciated the
schism within its soul, a schism that rent his own psyche, cursing
his relations with kith and kin and damning the very institutions whose doors were open to him only because he was a
preacher. This open door was the South's reward for the ministers who protected its mythos, in the celebrated fashion of the
Baptist preacher in Raleigh, Thomas Dixon, who authored *The
Klansman*. Woe to that preacher who deviated; he became a
marked man, a traitor to the region. This schism in the Southern
psyche was debilitating. One was to preach the grace of the radical Gospel and at the same time to preserve the rigidity of privilege for the white race. Thus the problem of racism for the white
minister was altogether different from that of the black minister.
When the black preacher condemned segregation he condemned
an acknowledged evil. Both the God he worshiped and the congregation he served concurred. When the black preacher sacri-

ficed himself on the altar of social activism, he was praised. When the white preacher took the same stand, he was ridiculed and, if not tarred and feathered, soon found himself without a pulpit. For fifty years Finlator tried to steer these perilous waters, assuring his black friends that he stood beside them in their struggle and assuring his white Southern friends that he was acting in their best interests. It was an impossible undertaking, and he could hardly expect to succeed.

In 1951, as chairman of the North Carolina Baptist Convention's Committee on Social Service and Civil Righteousness, Finlator had the rare opportunity to shape its report and to read it before the Convention meeting in Asheville. In a lengthy statement touching on eleven different topics, four of these pertained to race.

> Both as fellow citizens in a democracy and as fellow workers in Christ, the Negro has a claim upon us which has never been fully honored. That claim, stated simply, is to be accepted as a total person. In the new South that is in the making, a South of greater economic, industrial and educational opportunity, we are dealing with a new Negro. Far from the humble, amiable Uncle Tom many would fancy him, the Negro today is restive, proud, resentful, informed, ambitious and determined to bring to his race that same self-respect and elemental justice for which the founding fathers laid down their lives that we might enjoy. . . . It is for the churches to decide this hour whether their witness of universal brotherhood shall, in deference to tradition and convention, go unproclaimed while the Negro, though deeply religious, seeks his fulfillment in secular sources, on the other hand: or bravely to accept the challenge, and in the name of Him who died for all become a part of the adventure of love transcending every tradition and taboo that frustrate and defeat the Christian ethic in society.

Finlator proceeded to expose the problems of farm tenancy, of migrant workers, and of labor-management relations, all of which he interpreted as connected with racism. Lastly he exposed the Ku Klux Klan.

Many of the members of this organization are no doubt members also of Baptist churches. This lays upon our Baptist ministers and laymen a grave obligation. They must be willing to speak frankly against such un-American and un-Christian behavior and do their utmost to discredit the violent language and action that such groups invariably use in order to pursue ends, which however rationalized in terms of Americanism, are dangerously subversive of all social and religious good. They must also be willing to face and deal with the conditions and environments conducive to the spread of the Klan.

This report carries seeds that reach fruition in many of Finlator's later commitments. But as is often the fate of many sound ecclesiastical motions, his report was buried in "the noise of your solemn assemblies."

The Supreme Court ruling of 17 May 1954 rocked the churches and reinvigorated Negro aspirations. The initial official action of both the North Carolina Baptist Convention and the Southern Baptist Convention was to urge compliance as the Christian citizen's duty. At the SBC meeting in St. Louis, only two speakers rose against the motion to comply. This action turned out to be premature since within the immediately ensuing months massive resistance mounted throughout the South, not the least within many Baptist churches. Finlator took his pen in hand and reminded his brethren not to retreat. In an article, "Baptists are on Record," he masterfully summarized the official pronouncements of Baptists against racism dating from 1939. Then he challenged Baptists to take action.

A critical moment in history has put Southern Baptists existentially on the spot. No one has the slightest doubt that this critical moment is desegregation. The rulings of the Supreme Court affect chiefly that section of the nation where the largest number of our citizens are segregated and where Southern Baptists have the greatest number, wealth and influence. . . . Is it too much to say that in a large measure the future of the white race is in our hands? The decisions of the high court do not come as a surprise nor do they find us totally unprepared. . . . The eyes of the world, the eyes of the Lord, are upon us. The way will not be easy nor the burden light. But we have our Christian conscience, our faith in democracy, our loyalty to the Constitution and the official pronouncements of Baptist fellowship to bid us go forward.[2]

With this moral foundation for change within Southern culture, what kept the political structure of a desegregated society from rising more swiftly? Finlator, writing both as a loyal adherent of the Democratic Party and as a churchman, dispatched a public letter to Governor Luther Hodges on 4 August 1955, urging him to embrace desegregation publicly, based on compliance with the law. Finlator had just been to Europe in attendance at the Baptist World Alliance and he reminded the Governor of world opinion on this question. That Hodges was not enthusiastic is clear from his reply to Finlator on 8 August. "We treat them much better in this country, whereas in many countries they do a lot of theorizing but keep them down economically." (*Them* obviously refers to blacks.)

Sentiment was building both in the political arena and within the churches against compliance, and a climate of defensiveness within white Southern public opinion was congealing. In December 1955, in the city of Montgomery, Alabama, Rosa Parks's defiant act in refusing to move to segregated seating on a city bus catapulted Dr. Martin Luther King, Jr. into the national limelight and served ironically to advance those political and religious leaders who loudly resisted the Supreme Court.

Finlator assumed a lonely leadership within the Baptist community against these forces. In 1956, he persuaded the North Carolina Council of Churches to make a financial grant to support King's cause, a grant to the Montgomery Improvement Association. In 1958, he was elected to the Board of the Southern Conference Educational Fund, the one interracial organization within the South most promoting integration. In an open letter on 4 October 1958, he chided the Board of Trustees of Wake Forest University about that institution's racist admission policy.

---

[2]Finlator, "Baptists are on the Record," *Biblical Recorder* 121 (15 October 1955): 6.

Since the Baptist State Convention in 1955 decided to vest the boards of trustees of the seven Baptist colleges with complete authority to deal with the admission of Negroes, it must be assumed that the Director of Admissions at Wake Forest [September 23, AP release] was carrying out the wishes of the Wake Forest Board of Trustees. . . . It must be further assumed that in spite of the appearances of "local control" the Baptists of North Carolina, as far as their colleges are concerned, are offering "massive resistance."

In a state where for a number of years Negroes have been accepted at both graduate and undergraduate levels in the State universities and colleges and where the public schools are beginning to comply with the law against segregation, we are witnessing a strange reversal in the law-versus-grace dialectic. We Baptists are in effect saying through our Christian schools to the "secular" school: what you who live under law must accept, we who live under Grace may refuse—even if your accepting is by our standards Christian and our refusal by the same standards unchristian.

Meanwhile Finlator had become pastor of Pullen Memorial Church. Soon after arriving he took up the task that had begun under Dr. E. McNeil Poteat, that of completing a church constitution that would state formally that Pullen had an open-door policy for receiving members. After the 1954 decision, Dr. Poteat had urged the congregation to use Sunday School time, open forums and study courses to prepare the church membership for the social experiment of desegregation. He had been mortally shaken when he encountered stiff opposition to this concrete implementation of Christian brotherhood. Although Pullen had distinguished itself as a congregation that welcomed blacks to worship and had many members who in their private capacities were quite liberal on the matter, the church had not yet clarified its policy about admitting blacks to membership. Many members felt that the sudden, tragic death of Dr. Poteat made it possible to write into their constitution that any person subscribing to the general principles formulated by the church would be eligible for membership. That clause was accepted in March 1958. There was no rush of blacks for membership. The Pullen church, however, backed its new policy by joining the United Church, the Davie Presbyterian Church and two black churches to sponsor a totally integrated summer Bible school and camp. The churches were obliged to stage the camp by busing the pupils to a distant location, the black section of the segregated Umstead Public Park.

While Finlator continued to prod the Pullen congregation in these directions, he busied himself establishing friendships across racial lines with black preachers such as Charles Ward, Grady Davis, and Brezell Robinson and with civil rights lawyers such as Floyd McKissick, Julius Chambers, and James Ferguson. He taught classes at Shaw University from 1956 to 1960, during the period when the Student Nonviolent Coordinating Committee was organized on campus and when among his many students was Leon White, later to be the leading spokesman for civil rights among the churchmen of the state. He invited both black speakers and black choirs to participate in Pullen worship; among those filling the pulpit was Andrew Young. Such actions and periodic sermons on the subject raised only a few complaints, causing an occasional member to withdraw and an undetermined number of visitors to seek membership elsewhere. The story goes that a relative of a member chanced to be present on Reformation Sunday; seeing Martin Luther's name, she exclaimed, "Does he have to preach on that man every Sunday?" Still as pastor he had done very little to rock the boat. It was one thing to announce that "segregation is dead," to transcend its barriers by establishing friendships across racial lines, and to wait as a gradualist and a moderate for "the all deliberate speed" of the judicial process. It was quite another thing to lock arms in a black-and-white street protest, singing "We Shall Overcome," and to assert the policy affirmed by King, "The citizen can take direct action against injustice without waiting for the government to act or a majority to agree with him or her or a court to rule in his favor." Few if any white churches were prepared for the latter strategy and almost all lacked the heart to develop it.

When Finlator crossed the line from the one strategy to the other, in a series of pronouncements in the early 1960s, and backed these up with concrete actions, he was viewed by "moderate" whites as inflaming the atmosphere. His approval of the sit-ins, his public breakfast with the Freedom Riders, his apology for the urban riots, Black Power and the Black Manifesto, his feeding of the Poor People's Campaign marchers, his defense of Ben Chavis and the Wilmington Ten, his own marching alongside Angela Davis with the North Carolina Alliance Against Racism and Political Repression—these and a host of like actions caused him to be labeled as an enemy of the South and the white race. The white South, caught in the vise of the evertightening legal enforcement of desegregation, manifest in the Civil Rights Act of 1964 and the Voting Rights Act of 1965, and the dramatic aggressiveness of the blacks to cast off their shackles and claim their equality, became more and more defensive.

All of these events were just ahead when Finlator was invited by the Baptist association meeting in Henderson, North Carolina, on 25 October 1959. He was assigned the task of addressing specifically four major social crises. In attacking racism he gave evidence of a breakthrough beyond the traditional pattern of race relations. Linking economic exploitation and racial discrimination, he declared, "The two are inextricably interwoven and neither can be dealt with definitively apart from the other." He indicted the nation's political leadership for forging "an unholy alliance to trade antiunion support for anticivil rights support." Concluding the speech, he sounded for the first time the slogan "a desegregated church in a desegregated society."

With the coming of the 1960s the seriousness of his commitment to that principle would be tested, particularly in reference to the gubernatorial candidacy of his former college Sunday School teacher, I. Beverly Lake, and to the first sit-in staged in Greensboro. On 13 January 1960, Finlator issued a public letter denouncing Lake as a racist. On 27 March in a major article printed in the *News and Observer*, "What's Right, What's Wrong: An Appraisal of North Carolina for North Carolinians," he approved the sit-ins. Few ministers, not to speak of few citizens among the white population, dared endorse the sit-ins at this moment of history. Dean Foster Payne of Shaw University wrote to Finlator 5 April, in response to the newspaper article.

> Ever since the beginning of the protests by our students in
> Raleigh and other parts of North Carolina, I have expected and
> listened for the voices of fellow white leaders in support of our
> students. . . . There are reasons for their inaction in this regard—
> some day that story will be told.

Yes, twenty-five years later that story may be told, at least in part.
Liberal college presidents, such as Dr. Gordon Blackwell of the
University of North Carolina in Greensboro and Dr. Harold Tribble of Wake Forest University, where ten students had been arrested sitting-in with the black students at the local Woolworth
store on 23 February 1960, had discouraged white student participation. President Blackwell forbade his girls to be seen in the
vicinity where the sit-ins were occurring, and President Tribble
called his ten students together in the Trustee Room and reminded them that they had made their noise and had best return
to their primary business, academics.

Increasingly Finlator's public posture separated him from the
usual "white liberal." 1961 found him back in the headlines on
several matters: on 15 February he gave a speech before B'nai
B'rith in Greensboro in which he favored the new tactics of the
civil rights movement; on 27 October, he chaired the Southern
Conference Educational Fund meeting in Chapel Hill. On 27 May
1962 he was photographed while eating breakfast with the Freedom Riders in the Raleigh bus station. But more attention came
from a speech delivered at Shaw University on 14 February.
Headlined as "Padlock the Restaurants," his address suggested
that instead of arresting students for wanting to buy a ham-
burger, public officials should padlock any public eating place that
refused to serve the public. With the press coverage of his sermon
on the same topic on 19 August 1962, the floodwaters of public
wrath finally spilled over. Of the scores of letters of abuse written
to him, four provide some sampling of the arguments.

> Instead of preaching about sins of people and trying to save
> souls, you are trying to get your name in the paper. You like so
> many other so-called preachers are getting away from the Bible,
> I think, and are trying to win favor of people. God made all of us

our individual colors and I personally feel that God didn't intend for us to mix.

Just a few suggestions on how you may advance your cause for integration: 1. Build a chain of restaurants and call them "Finlator Color Bar" 2. Leave your present congregation and go to Grace's Mission on East Street. 3. Don't forget your giant-size deodorant. 4. Better still join the Mau Mau. I know of one man that is the same brand as you. Judas.

Two things come to mind: How many Negroes were present in your church to hear what you had to say? And, how many Negroes live in your residential section?

In my opinion, this man has amply illustrated his lack of suitability for the position he holds and has forfeited the respect that might ordinarily attend his ministry.

In forwarding to Finlator the clipping of this last letter, its author wrote, "Actually two things should be padlocked: your mouth and your church as long as you are pastor."

There were a few letters of commendation. Harry Jones, executive secretary of the North Carolina Human Relations Council, wrote from Charlotte on 27 August, "We have nothing but silence from the ministers here as far as the restaurant issue is concerned. More power to you, Bill."

What Finlator actually said in those speeches of 15 February and 19 August 1962 can scarcely be considered to be breaking new ground, since they were fully in accord with his lifelong defense of the rights of every American citizen. Such is the line, "I commend those many courageous young people, both white and colored, whose heinous crime of daring to be Americans (for ultimately that is the meaning behind the sit-ins and the freedom riders) has landed them in jail." What his critics ostensibly found intolerable was that a Christian minister could commend persons who broke the law and who though professing nonviolence constantly provoked violence by their tactics aimed at removing the color bar. Incidentally, the opposition originated not solely among diehard Southern racists. Paul Ramsey, at that moment Protestantism's leading ethicist, teaching at Princeton, published his book opposing King's methods, *Christian Ethics and the Sit-ins,* in 1961. Finlator's position was even more rare when viewed from the ranks of Southern Baptists. How far he was ahead of the pack is now documented by an official history of Southern Baptists who participated in promoting interracialism, published in 1978 and entitled *Their Heart is Black.* Not a single person featured in the book was a public advocate of integration during the 1960s nor did one of them participate personally with King and the freedom movement.

At the moment not even Finlator had joined a sit-in. He was introduced to the experience by a few members of his own church. Walking Fayetteville Street, the main thoroughfare of Raleigh, almost daily was a mixed group protesting the Jim Crow policies of its theatres and restaurants, among whom were Dr. L. E. M. Freeman, Professor Lawrence Highfill and Bob Pritchard of the Pullen Church. They enlisted their pastor in June 1963. In November of that year, Finlator drove east to the little village of Williamston where several Northern clergymen who had joined with Golden Frinks of the Southern Christian Leadership Conference were thrown in jail. There he visited American Baptist ministers Paul Stagg and Harvey Cox. Both wrote letters thanking him for his visit and affirming that he was the only local Southern white minister to take note of their plight.

On 17 July 1963 he addressed an open letter to Senators Everett Jordan and Sam Ervin, urging them to endorse forthrightly civil rights for all.

> You, Senators Ervin and Jordan, do not really belong in the same camp with the Eastlands and Thurmonds with their messianic complex to pull down like Samson of old the pillars of society and who seem prepared to do just this, if only they can prevent the twentieth century from happening.
>
> Do not hesitate to part company with them. You have powerful allies on the other side. Consider what the mayors and businessmen and civic leaders across our state are now doing. These people are your constituents and they have the support of our citizenry.
>
> Listen to the pronouncements of every major religious body in our country and state. Ponder the growing national conscience against the injustice and disabilities imposed for generations

upon a great segment of our people. True statesmanship from you
will, as I have said, receive wide and spontaneous support
throughout our state. Who knows how many other state leaders
may be waiting for this act of courage to identify themselves with
you?

Although Finlator and Ervin were strict constitutional adherents, over the years Finlator became a thorn in Ervin's side on
matters pertaining to race and sex. In a public letter to the *Charlotte Observer,* published 4 August 1966, Finlator challenged the
designation of a person's race on state marriage licenses, and enlisted Ervin's assistance in striking it from the law books. Ervin
replied on 8 August, "There are two reasons I cannot do this. One,
I will not involve myself in state affairs. Two, I do not favor mis-
cegenation."

Finlator's outspoken crusade on behalf of minorities became
his hallmark as a political parson. During the 1970s when he was
appointed Chairman of the North Carolina Advisory Committee
to the U.S. Civil Rights Commission, he led that group over a ten-
year span to conduct five major investigations, all bearing on racism. What he pioneered during the 1960s fitted him for that
unique leadership. Whether he was appraising "the Baptist image" (1 September 1964), defining "the New South" in an address
to the College Young Democrats (7 May 1965), challenging the
North Carolina AFL-CIO Convention to integrate (20 September
1965), blasting the Vietnam war (28 February 1965), or defending the National Council of Churches (1 November 1965), Finlator somehow got around to exposing racism.

It is true that during the late 1960s his time would be
preempted by protests against the war. But if he did not know how
vitally the two problems were joined, he soon discovered for himself. In a public letter to the *Charlotte Observer,* on 4 July 1967
he defended Muhammad Ali, the champion heavyweight boxer,
in his refusal to be drafted. White response was violent. Black response is typified by a letter dated 10 July 1967.

      Thank you for the letter on Muhammad Ali which appeared
recently in "The People's Forum."

It was a masterpiece. More than that, it expressed precisely the feeling of the Negro community. Most Negroes, whether they say so or not, now have a deep admiration for this young man. They appreciate his rigid discipline of the physical body, his high moral standards . . . and his dedication to the religious principles of his faith.

Many of us feel that this young man's strong convictions have exposed much of the hypocrisy of the time.

During the same period, Finlator was obliged to come to the defense of Martin Luther King, Jr., who in April 1967 had made his first public broadside against the Vietnam war and the American nation "for being the most immoral country in the world." A Baptist editorial in the 13 April issue of *Charity and Children* voiced the prevailing public opinion that King had best "restrict his crusades to civil rights and uplifting the minority groups in this country." Finlator wrote to the editor on 18 May,

A bit further on the editorial refers to the occasion "when King steps out of his accustomed role" in criticizing the involvement of our country in Vietnam. Obviously such statements convey a feeling that Dr. King, as an American citizen, ought to confine his concerns and activities. Is this not a vestige of segregationism when we make up our minds that a certain man is doing legitimate business as long as he remains "in his place"? . . . In such statements as these the editorial seems to be commending Dr. King for his leadership in bringing about peaceful change and for his consistent opposition to violence. Yet when Dr. King applies this same attitude toward his own government at the level in Washington the editorial makes him a "peace at any cost" advocate.

It may be there is a vital message at the heart of all this that we fail to get. Could there possibly be an analogy to the use of violence and intimidation and threats, say in the Mississippi delta by sheriffs and Ku Klux Klansmen and landlords on the one hand and, on the other hand, the use of phosphorous and napalm bombs on another peasant people eight thousand miles away?

Hardly had the public furor over his defense of Muhammad Ali died down when Finlator, invited to address the North Carolina Conference of Christians and Jews on 15 August 1967, pre-

sented what many listeners took to be a sympathetic rationale for
the current burning of the inner cities of America. In "The Hier-
oglyphics of Violence," he began by asking his audience "to think
about deciphering the fearful code of communication that lies at
the heart, as I believe, of the rioting, the looting, and the shooting
that have ravished our cities during the past weeks." Then he
moved to the core of his argument.

> Violence [is excused in America] to achieve national policy but
> no violence [is excused in America] to achieve human dignity at
> home.
>
> Black power has come to stay. We have asked for it. This is
> the nemesis on our premises and our only recourse is to live with
> it patiently and gracefully, accept it as a kind of penance, and
> binding our efforts to see to it that it is more a creative than a
> destructive force in our life . . . to hear what Negroes are trying
> to say with violence before it comes again. . . . It is not that other
> lines of communication have broken down. In simple truth, there
> never was any genuine communication to break down.

One newspaper carried the story with the headline, "Riots Defended." Many letter writers attacked Finlator bitterly for appearing to side with black extremists, but more moderate critics
wondered how a clergyman so well-known for his antiwar stand
and for being against handguns could now "excuse" the violence
of blacks.

In October 1967 he was back in the news again, this time for
supporting the garbage workers and their grievances against the
city of Raleigh. This strike was to drag on for months, during
which time Finlator continuously appealed to the city council and
the mayor to respond to their needs. On 5 February 1968, his sermon was devoted to housing in which he focused on real estate
discrimination and the plight of the poor. His sermon on the Sunday in April following King's death drew a massive congregation,
with many visitors who knew of the ties between Finlator and
King seeking some consolation for their own loss. King's last letter to Finlator had arrived just two weeks before the assassination.

All the while the animosity toward Finlator's concentration on racism was mounting among some members of his congregation. When Finlator persuaded the Pullen Church to help feed the Poor People's Campaign marchers as they came through Raleigh on their way to Washington in the summer following King's death, some of them took this as the last straw. Tolerance and civil rights were "all right," but attacking America's foreign policy and siding with the restless poor, vivified in the drama of the marchers eating in their own church, became the breaking point for a few diehards and disaffected others who were moderately inclined. One member wrote a letter on the occasion of withdrawing his membership.

> It is with much thought and deliberation that I have reached the following decision. This is not easy because we have been members of Pullen since we came to Raleigh in 1946. Both of my children were baptized at Pullen, so naturally we have had a rather close feeling for this church. . . . In spite of all this, I find it impossible to condone some of the completely radical and narrow ideas of our minister. Neither can I understand why our deacons agreed with our minister's policy to invite and feed in our church some of the participants of the Poor People's March. These people advocate anarchy and to a great extent are communist inspired. It is common knowledge that their leaders offered white students money and all the sex they desired if they would join their march. With such decadent principles as this, I just cannot conceive of any church condoning such acts.

The growing militancy of blacks may have reached a head when the Black Manifesto was produced in Detroit in April 1969, and dramatically introduced to the nation by James Foreman's abrupt interruption of the morning worship of the Riverside Church in New York City on 4 May 1969. Recognizing the crucial nature of the event, Finlator went before the annual convention of the North Carolina Baptists, meeting in Fayetteville on 11-12 November, with a resolution endorsing the principle if not the particulars of the Manifesto. In a lengthy but eloquent preliminary statement to the resolution, he appealed to the reparation motif as it appears in the Bible, in the Judeo-Christian tradition, in both the current Catholic sources and the World Council of

Churches, and in American history, specifically in Abraham Lincoln and the Bill of Rights. Trying carefully to avoid what he knew to be the inflammatory word, "reparations," he concluded,

> In the light of this rich heritage of Bible and church and state be it therefore resolved that the Baptists of North Carolina, whose lot has been cast in so goodly a heritage, shall strive together the more abundantly to extend to others what we so richly enjoy; that we acknowledge with sorrow the injustices and deprivations suffered by millions of our fellow citizens through the years and to this day and our involvement therein; and that out of our own free will and volition now more firmly and positively to make restitution as befits those to whom has been given the ministry of reconciliation. "Behold, Lord," said Zacchaeus, "the half of my goods I give to the poor, and if I have defrauded anyone of any thing, I restore it fourfold."

The resolution was referred to the Resolutions Committee and its members, without taking note of its relation to the Black Manifesto and without identifying the victims as the black citizens of America, altered the wording so that the impact of the word "reparations" returned to the resolution. The irony was not lost on Finlator. The resolution, as finally approved, reads:

> We now move firmly and positively to repair such damage to our relationship as possible, to break down barriers, that we walk together in brotherly love, and to heal the hurts of humanity through the ministry of reconciliation.

By contrast, the Southern Baptist Convention meeting the same year flatly rejected any attempt to get Baptists to respond as the Black Manifesto had demanded of the major Christian denominations.

Finlator was not alone in detecting the insertion of the concept "reparations" by the official Resolutions Committee. Six months afterwards an alarm was sounded about the implications of such a concept. B. J. Collins, in his 4 April 1970 letter to the *Recorder,* warned of the consequences for the denomination.

> You point out the financial troubles of the Episcopalians and their sharp division over their grant to the Malcolm X Libera-

tion University, along with financial troubles of the Presbyterians. I might add that the Methodists have also had trouble. . . .
As Baptists, this should be a good lesson to see that the same things do not happen to us.

Last November the convention passed a "Resolution on Restitution" which was an amended form of one proposed by W. W. Finlator. Probably few realize the significance of this resolution. The main difference between the original proposal and the amended one seems to be the last part [which now reads] "to repair such damage to our relationship as possible" [etc]

With this wording, it seems the State Convention's Budget Committee would be free to use our money in any number of ways including financial gifts to the Malcolm X Liberation University or any other militant group.

Marse Grant, editor of the *Recorder,* agreed. "The point is well-taken. As tight as money is right now, we believe we can say there is no chance of special allocations being made to any project like this by the State Convention." The voice of officialdom had won once again over the ethic of the Gospel. Jesse Helms, then editorial commentator for station WRAL-TV, Raleigh, also caught on. He editorialized on 20 November 1969,

The slumbering Convention, being against "injustice" as long as nobody bothers with a specific definition of it, yawned and nodded its approval of a watered-down version of the Finlator resolution. It was, all in all, a barely audible bit of sound without fury, signifying nothing. . . . It is worth the paper upon which it is written, and no more.

Helms missed the irony that this was one Finlator resolution that had not been watered down!

By 1970 Finlator was accustomed to participating in street demonstrations with both the anti-Vietnam forces and the labor unions. Later he was in the forefront of the ERA marchers. His first major march with blacks occurred on 8 January 1970 when he joined Coretta Scott King and others to protest the death penalty imposed on Marie Hill, an eighteen-year-old black girl languishing on death row at the North Carolina Central Prison. For the next decade he was the most visible white person in protests

by blacks. Sometimes these protests pertained to blacks imprisoned under questionable indictments and judicial procedure, as
with the Wilmington Ten and the Charlotte Three; sometimes
they pertained to the lack of thoroughgoing integration within the
public schools; sometimes it was a single issue, as with the government's disposal of PCB-contaminated soil in Warren County,
where blacks composed the largest proportion of the population;
in 1976 he paraded with the North Carolina Alliance Against
Racism and Political Repression, alongside Angela Davis, who,
like himself, addressed the crowd. These events, well covered by
the press, kept him identified as a friend of blacks and succeeded
in making him the target of the ire of narrow-minded whites.

In the process he accumulated a host of black friends. Besides
the black ministers cited earlier in this chapter, his close friends
included the leader of Negro Baptists, O. L. Sherrill, and activist
ministers such as Leon White, Ben Chavis and Golden Frinks.
Politicians such as the Spauldings and Wheelers of Durham and
A. J. Turner of Raleigh were counted among his friends. With
Finlator's appointment to the chairmanship of the North Carolina Advisory Committee on Civil Rights in 1971 his contacts
within the minority community enlarged immensely, and likewise his established credibility considerably enhanced the effectiveness of that organization as it attempted to be "the eyes and
ears" of the citizenry in reporting any violations of civil rights to
the Justice Department. Finlator also belonged to the Urban
League and was often the featured speaker at black functions. In
particular, the North Carolina Medical Association, the General
Baptist Convention, and the North Carolina Association of Education frequently invited him to speak. He received the "Citizen
of the Year" award from the Raleigh black community in 1967 and
1976, and in May 1981 the two black leaders who had labored for
years alongside Finlator in the Advisory Committee, Edith Ham-
mond and Tommie Young, chaired a testimonial banquet in his
honor. On that occasion, Floyd McKissick, one of the valedictory
speakers, recounted how his neighbor, upon hearing of his driv-
ing to Raleigh to honor a white friend, exclaimed, "Why, law me!
I didn't know that man was white. I always thought he was black
just like us."

Finlator's drooping spirits were encouraged by this black support, something he found very much lacking within the white community. He seemed to find himself in freer, more compatible surroundings and thoroughly enjoyed the company. Examining his speeches before black audiences, one gets the impression that he spoke his convictions more readily and more vigorously in their presence. Black Baptist preachers were less restrained by ecclesiastical control than Southern Baptist preachers; they were also more likely to be ecumenically minded and to address social issues.

One example of Finlator's use of this freer forum is his exposure of the censorship practiced by a Southern Baptist agency in withholding from distribution a publication that pictured on the cover a black and white teen-ager sitting together. The title of the church periodical was "Becoming." On the platform provided by the General Baptist Convention in 1971, Finlator decried such fear of the truth. Another example is his response to the invitation to join the group Mobilization Against Racism on 12 November 1974.

> It is a privilege and an honor to join other concerned citizens in a vigorous and committed and peaceful demonstration of our faith that America belongs to all of us and in a ringing affirmation that we stand against racism. . . . Sign me, minister in the Southern Baptist Convention living in Raleigh.

The minority groups of North Carolina returned his affection; they appreciated the courage demanded of a white minister exercising the role undertaken by Finlator. Both blacks and the Lumbee Indians (the largest body of Indians east of the Mississippi) rallied to his side during his tenure as chairman of the State Advisory Committee. They sensed "a friend in high places." They counted on his good offices for any redress and shared Finlator's high opinion of the committee during that period. In Finlator's 1977 letter to President Carter he maintained that this Committee is "the only national group that has possessed in recent days the courage sharply to challenge the administration for certain policies and attitudes regarding minority groups." Under his leadership all five public hearings conducted by the Committee—on public schools, the Robeson Indians, prison conditions, migrant labor, and the Greensboro killings of 1979—related in some way to overcoming racism.

A letter from the Rev. Wilson Lee, pastor of St. John Baptist Church, Statesville, expressed the depth of black affection for Finlator. Mr. Lee wrote in appreciation for Finlator's quick response when his home was riddled with bullets in what Mr. Lee thought was an attempt by the Ku Klux Klan to intimidate him for his long record of working for equal rights.

> There is an old Negro spiritual which says, "He may not come when you want him, but when He comes, He is right on time." I think this expression is befitting of you and our relationship. You are right on time and have been over the years. We thank you from the depth of our hearts for the great work you have done for us, all of us.

Finlator had begun his civil rights campaign out of a sense of fairness and of devotion to the American legal system, but he ended in love with those members of the minorities he had labored for and alongside of. In an article, "Memories of a Grand and Awful Time," written at the request of the *Winston-Salem Journal,* he confessed,

> I have no way of adequately expressing my indebtedness to black leaders. I can only point out to my friends in other liberation movements that, without the leadership of blacks, the rest of us would not have gotten off the ground. I am thinking not only of the dauntless black civil rights leaders but of those many black preachers who have had me in their churches, traveled with me as comrades, held meetings and drawn up resolutions and raised banners.[3]

But beyond what he called his "passion for civil rights being home bred," in his native sense of equity and fairness rooted in participatory democracy, was his understanding of God as the supreme agent of reconciliation. In his sermon for 19 January 1969, "Top Drawer Priorities," he put first

---

[3]Finlator, "Memories of a Grand and Awful Time," *Winston-Salem* (NC) *Journal,* 30 July 1982, 8.

the reconciliation of the races. This is our number one assignment and nothing presses us with more urgency. Reconciliation
means equality of opportunity and justice at all levels. It means
the abolition of old laws and ordinances that inhibit justice and
the enactment of new laws that promote it. It means in short, the
commitment of the moral and legal authority towards the removal of the last vestige of racism throughout the land.

In the same year, he was quoted in the fall issue of the *Raleigh
Magazine,*

Reparations for black people could be a healthy thing and it
could have spiritual value. I don't go around wallowing in ances-
tral guilt, but I think after 300 years of maltreatment, reparations are in order. What the black person needs is for the white
man to say, we did it, we know we did it, and this is a way of saying we're sorry we did it. And the white man needs it too, because
that is the way he can be a joyous part of the reconciliation that
we Christians must have.

Speaking in 1970 to the Good Neighbor Council of Wallace on
the subject, "The Church and Race Relations," Finlator emphasized the church's failure. "No one can deal fairly with the church
and race relations," he said "without confessing at the outset that
the church has in the past blessed, sanctioned and supported the
institution of slavery and segregation." To him this was the added
tragedy of so many Baptist churches joining the rush to establish
"Christian academies" in an obvious attempt to circumvent desegregation of public schools.

Finlator viewed the public school system as the mainstay of
democracy. His first job as chairman of the Civil Rights Committee was to preside over hearings of the progress of desegregation
in education, held in four area cities of the state in the spring of
1971. In that very summer the Raleigh system was facing the
tensions accompanying its newly initiated plan for complete integration, or what is called "racial balancing." Finlator tried to
prepare his own congregation with a special word on July 24.

We are living, as the hymn reminds us, in a grand and awful
time, a time when, like our Saviour, we must go about *doing* good.

If others withdraw their children and send them to private
schools, accept this with deep regret and quiet sorrow, but pledge
yourself with renewed vigor to support the public schools.

As an example, and quite contrary to what some of his "liberal"
friends did, his own children remained enrolled during the desegregation hassle, and Mrs. Finlator lent her own constructive
efforts as a public school teacher.

As for the so-called "Christian academies," most of which were
utilizing the facilities provided by churches, especially Baptist
churches, Finlator had nothing but contempt. His best analysis
of them was given in a letter to the editor of the *News and Observer,* on 25 August 1969, but it received a much wider audience
in a national journal, *The Baptist Program,* under the title,
"Please Don't Call It Christian."

> Just at the time when our public schools are required by law
> to exercise courageous and imaginative compliance there are
> mushrooming up across the state institutions ostensibly under
> the auspices of the church with the real, if not avowed, purpose
> of evading the compliance requirement. That these little bas-
> tions of final resistance can get money and support is not sur-
> prising. They hold out some hope of white separatism. But do you
> know what they are calling themselves? Christian academies!
> The very heart and genius of the Christian witness is inclusive-
> ness and brotherhood and mutual acceptance and reconciliation,
> yet here are academies of exclusiveness and separation that dare
> call themselves "Christian" and are getting away with it.[4]

Simultaneously the federal administration seemed to be
backtracking in its pursuit of integration in public schools. President Nixon had decided to withhold federal funds that might be
used in busing children for the purpose of achieving racial balance. Supporting the editor of the *Recorder* for scoring Nixon,
Finlator wrote on 19 August 1971,

> The American people, in my judgement, are at the point of ac-
> cepting the falsity of "separate but equal education." We know

---

[4]Finlator, "Please Don't Call It Christian," *The Baptist Program* (June 1970):
8.

that neither quality nor equality can be achieved for all under a system of segregated schooling. At this point in our national life integration in the schools can only come through some form of busing. The President has rendered a great disservice to our efforts toward harmony and community in this critical hour. I am grateful for the strong witness of the Recorder in unmasking this.

In November 1972, Finlator took the floor of the Baptist State Convention to offer a resolution that came to be called "A Plea for Public Schools." It passed.

> Because of our deep concern (1) over the increasing pressure for government support of parochial and private schools in other communions, and (2) the use of resources and facilities in our own fellowship in support of Christian academies and other similar institutions, be it resolved that the North Carolina Baptist Convention, meeting in Winston-Salem on November 14, 1972, reaffirm its faith in the public schools and call upon our Baptist people to give their undivided support and encouragement to the achievement of quality education to all the children of North Carolina.

The public school system of America had become the battle ground for the opposing forces, and opposition to "busing" had become the latest code word to disguise the recalcitrant. To Finlator it seemed ever so plain. In a letter to the *News and Observer* on 22 September 1972, he made his position known.

> Busing is no longer a word but an emotion. . . . Yet busing has been around a rather long time, 50 years to be precise. . . . The American people are fundamentally committed to the cherished principle of quality education for all of our children and must not, and ultimately will not, be deterred from this achievement by appeals to fear and prejudice and hate—all wrapped up in that little word busing.

But what was self-evident to Finlator was becoming ominously confusing to others, especially those who did not share his understanding of the Gospel and the American Constitution. Integration had become a questionable concept, sullied not only in the eyes of many whites but now rejected by many aggressive blacks. The latter's disillusion with the concept was registered in the publicized disagreement between Stokely Carmichael and Martin Luther King on their Mississippi walk in the wake of the wounding of James Meredith in the summer of 1966. For one thing, it was a one-way street. Even Finlator did not urge joining black churches. Whites did not move to black ghettos, and generally it was the few privileged blacks who were accepted in the suburbs. Liberal whites who promoted integration, regardless of how much personal liability they took, seldom risked everything.

Many whites faced with the loss of their neighborhood schools (something that had happened earlier for blacks under the first steps toward integration) and with the inconvenient busing of their children, with quotas and affirmative action, with the takeover of certain inner cities and concomitantly certain public school systems by blacks, were having second thoughts about continued legal leverage to alleviate racism. What was once a simple "right and wrong" issue was no longer viewed so simplistically. Particularly the "white liberals" who had pursued solutions provided by law were rudely awakening to the reality that human beings do not live by law alone. Finlator, of all persons, was not unaware of this blacklash sweeping the white community. He summarized the new mood: "Racism has altered its face, but it is still with us." What he hardly anticipated was that his own victimization in the struggle would come not from the ranks of the bigots, the rednecks and the uneducated, but from the "liberals" within his own camp, some of whom were quite proud of their own integration record.

Over the years Finlator had fought white prejudice at different levels. At the beginning of his ministry he had dared preach the mere acceptance of the black person as a human. Progressively he moved to abolish segregation itself. With the appearance of King and the freedom movement, involving direct action and disobedience of unjust laws, he followed suit. By the time of the Black Power advocates and the burning of the inner cities and their demand for reparations, he was able to provide a rationale even for that behavior. Successively he was viewed by the white community as moving further out on a limb. Cheap prejudice reiterated its charge of "nigger lover"; more sophisticated prejudice asserted that "Bill would rationalize anything the blacks do."

Finlator's enemies in his battle against racism had always been many and they had been powerful, but for nearly fifty years he had managed to escape the noose. This time they would not lose their opportunity. The tragedy is that the locus of the crushing blow was his own congregation. He was obliged to resign from the one platform he had so stoutly and consistently boasted was the the freest in the South. In the end, the freedom he claimed for it was repudiated by the way it muzzled him.

What precipitated the crisis within the Pullen Church was the telegram that Finlator, as chairman of the North Carolina Advisory Committee on Civil Rights, sent to the President of the United States on 23 March 1979. Its language conformed to Finlator's lifelong stand against racism, nothing sensational. "You are urgently requested to take administrative action to end illegal segregation in higher education. The North Carolina Advisory Committee is deeply concerned that high regard and strict compliance with federal law shall prevail in our state." Finlator's customary appeal was manifest: segregation is illegal, laws must be obeyed, and the authority implicit in a citizen review. Yet it fell like a bombshell on his Pullen congregation. True, he demanded that the federal government cut off its allocation to the University system—eighty-nine million dollars expected within the year—if it continued any racial discrimination. Many members were employed by or had family ties in the University system.

For a quarter of century their pastor had railed against racism; and, while his outspokenness had rubbed some members the wrong way, the majority stuck by him, and, indeed, could be counted as allies in the fight against racism. Yet such a storm of objection from certain influential members bombarded the Board of Deacons that by the following spring that controlling body demanded an early retirement. Reliable sources report that little more than one half of the 24-member Board was present and that both the chair and vice-chair were absent. Finlator, faced with the undesired cessation of his ministry to a congregation, the majority of whose members he was led to believe still wanted him as their pastor, faced a hard decision. He judiciously bowed out by announcing that his retirement date would be 30 June 1982, one year later than the Board had requested.

Outwardly, Finlator took his forced retirement philosophically. In fact, one could go further and apply the word so often used to characterize Finlator by persons close to him, watching him perform under pressure: he took it *graciously*. But that he was hurt, and hurt deeply, is putting it mildly. Racism was hardly the issue that he had expected to defeat him in the end. Certainly the Pullen congregation was not expected to use this particular weapon. Many years before, Lloyd Preslar in a journalistic profile in the *Winston-Salem Journal,* had surmised that "Finlator is well aware that his open outspokenness may cost him position within the church. 'But the word "success" is not in the New Testament,' he said. 'The only thing the Bible says is that you've got to be faithful. The Bible says, "Proclaim the truth."'"[5] That the 1979 telegram would cost him his position in the *Pullen* church, and that he paid such a price so *late* in his career, these were hardly in his crystal ball. In the aftermath, Finlator, who had always been so free with the press, remained close-mouthed. The opposing faction insisted that the telegram was but a small part of a larger problem, namely Finlator's tendency to concentrate his pulpit ministry on social justice. Their disclaimer is belied, however, by a reading of the scores of letters that both the Board and Finlator received during the dispute.

Finlator answered each letter inquiring about the circumstances of his "forced" retirement, but never in detail. Typical of his reserve is a letter to Dr. Arthur Kale, on 1 August 1980, in the very middle of the dispute.

> We are indeed saddened over the turn of events and your letter indicates that you are aware of the complexities that are involved. This wonderful group of Pullen folks have put up with me for twenty-four years and I could have survived, with the ministry I have, nowhere else in the south, or at least in no other Southern Baptist church. I would like sometime to talk with you at length about it and fill you more in on a distressful and still

---

[5]Lloyd Preslar, "Fighting Baptist Liberal," *Winston-Salem* (NC) *Journal,* 7 February 1960, 7.

exciting situation. Perhaps one of the most difficult dimensions is the fact that the people who are insisting on a date for retirement are long standing personal friends and people who truly love Pullen Memorial. So there! Nonetheless there seems to be strong support throughout the congregation for the kind of ministry I have brought here. Thus the matter transcends me, which it ought, and it becomes a matter of the church deciding on certain principles regarding itself. Wow!

The St. Petersburg (Florida) *Times* on 20 September 1980 quoted Finlator as saying, "There are some who think the university issue is the cause. . . . It has not been mentioned at all. But I know my action did create a great deal of discomfort; it shook up many people more than anything I have ever done."

Racism had finally taken its revenge on Finlator. Over the years he had somehow managed to escape violence to his person, cross-burnings on his lawn, bombings of his home, acid thrown on his children, curses to his wife, but at last it took his job, a position he had handcrafted into a celebrated example of the free and responsible pulpit in America. The South, which had traditionally used the race question to settle its score with its rebellious sons, had claimed one more proud victim.

In the wake of this tragedy, Finlator was obliged to rethink his own philosophy of liberalism and his unique ministry of social action. Could it be that his kind of liberalism was passé? Perhaps the causes for which he had put his life on the firing line had been won, but "won" in a way different from what he had expected. Issues such as desegregation, unionism, ecumenicity—all the causes of his youthful ministry—were being interpreted quite differently in his latter years. In the halcyon days of desegregation the public schools were destined to be even more the melting pot for democracy and the center of quality education; in the "winning" these goals were apparently lost. In an interview on 17 July 1981, Finlator responded on this point.

The issues that I have dealt with are not passé. They have not been "won." They are still very much with us. I am reminded of the statement that Christianity has not been given centuries to succeed and has failed—Christianity has never been fully tried.

There are more blacks today in segregated schools than before 1954. The Voting Rights Act is being opposed, the Ku Klux Klan is on the rise, and now nationwide, and the political power of the nation, including both senators from North Carolina, is striking down the legislation of decades designed primarily to lift the blacks, the women and the minorities. I have on the whole fought a losing fight and I fortify myself by facing the New Testament command that we are not to grow weary in well doing. I am pleased to see that these things have been the concern of my ministry across the years. I only wish that I had addressed them more vigorously and added to the list!

The happy warrior, now bruised and wiser, was still on the field of battle.

Chapter Five

MAKING PEACE

PEACE IS A CONSUMING INTEREST in the latter half of Finlator's life. By the time of his retirement he was involved in all kinds of peace work. In 1983 alone he led the Ft. Bragg protests against the training of Central American troops, went on a peace mission to Russia, spoke against nuclear weaponry, called for the reduction of military spending, lectured to religious peace groups, called for the U.S. approval of the antigenocide pact, and argued against the peacetime draft, among other things. By now he had become recognized as a major catalyst in prodding Southern Baptists toward support of peace initiatives, and nationwide he could be counted on to be one Southern Baptist preacher for any protest against America's "warring madness." The position he had finally formulated for himself may be derived both from a sermon and from a lecture dating from his retirement. "On the issue of peace there is no middle ground any more," Finlator declared in a sermon on 9 May 1982,

and my choice is between survival and annihilation. I can see for
the first time the terrible urgency of the command of Moses to the
Israelites to choose between life and death. That choice is not between a free world and a slave world, not between Christ and
Marx, not between national security and terrorism. It is between
life for all of us or death for all of us. All the old arguments of the
church to justify war go by the board. No war is just; no war is
winnable; no war can confine itself to the troops; no war can be
localized; no war can produce more good than evil; no war can restrict its ravages on any basis of proportionality. The possibility
of a nuclear be-all and end-all has swept all of these rationali-
zations away. In fact, there is no such thing as war any more; it
is only total annihilation.

Finlator's lecture was one of a series on Clarence Jordan delivered at Southern Baptist Theological Seminary in the spring of
1983. Jordan, next to Martin Luther King, Jr., was the century's
most celebrated Baptist pacifist.

It was a threat to the system to have a man in the heart of
fire-eating, saber-rattling South who sought peace and pursued
it. Violence had always been a way of life. How do you enforce
segregation laws, keep out labor unions and control the migrant
workers without violence? How do you maintain in the nation a
warfare economy or regulate the governments of other nations,
say in Central America, without the principle of violence? And
here was this man of peace challenging by his very presence 100%
Americanism!

Finlator's commitment to checking the military growth of
America, its movement toward a garrison-state economy and its
reliance on arms in its relations to the rest of the world came di-
rectly from his reading of the Sermon on the Mount with its
"Blessed are the peace makers," and from the example of Jesus,
"the Prince of Peace." Nevertheless, he never embraced pacifism.
Only with regard to nuclear warfare was he an absolute pacifist.
And his peace witness drew no national attention until his 1965
call for withdrawal from Vietnam in a public telegram to President Johnson. (This act came two years before Dr. King's crucial
speech of April 1967 in which he labeled America "the world's

greatest purveyor of violence.") Finlator backed that call by becoming one of the few Southern ministers, perhaps the only Baptist, to help organize Clergy and Laity Concerned about Vietnam, to stand protesting at the Pentagon gates, and to join the silent vigils on the streets of the state capitol.

Not until 1970 was he able to persuade a handful of other Southern Baptist ministers to cosign with him a resolution to put before the church convention. That resolution against the war was flatly rejected. In an interview given some years afterwards, appropriately titled "War Wounds," he reflected on the adverse conditions: "In the early days those of us who opposed the war felt very isolated."[1] The big names in American Christianity were blessing the (undeclared) war; they included both Cardinal Spellman and Billy Graham. In a speech as early as July 1966, entitled, "World Peace: A Spiritual Imperative," (subsequently published in several journals) he drew attention to this anomaly.

> How sad and yet how fitting to place the Cardinal and the Baptist evangelist with the leading Hawks of the American foreign policy! For, don't you see, Dr. Graham and Cardinal Spellman, that this means napalm bombs, defoliation, destruction of crops, murder of civilians and the growing possibility of genocide and a third world war and all in the name of God and freedom and peace.

Very little in Finlator's background—in his family, his education, or his Baptist affiliation—prepared him for this role in his mature years. Instead of hatred for war and love of peace, the South he grew up in had a romance with militarism. It was a machoculture, distinguishing itself with its chauvinistic patriotism and its volunteers for the country's military crusades and its tendency to identify America's goals with Christian goals.

Finlator was obliged to search for resources within his Southern and Baptist heritage that might make for peace. As evidenced by his earliest articulation of the problem he was acutely aware of the contradiction between his own church's stance and the way of Christ on the question of war and peace. He dug up the

---

[1]Quoted in "War Wounds," *Raleigh* (NC) *Times,* 2 May 1975, 11.

pacifist strain from the Anabaptist side of his denomination's history. In his *Christian Century* article of 6 April 1983, he noted, "Caught in the cross fires of the wars between Catholic and Protestant church states and heartily despised and feared by both, the early Baptists invoked a pox on both their houses. . . . They discouraged military service." Speaking at Southeastern Seminary in 1982, he said, "We can remind our flocks of the position of early Baptists on war, how they refused to take up arms—pacifists, objectors!" Nearly forty years previously, writing the editorial for the first edition of *Christian Frontiers,* in January 1946, he had appealed to the same Anabaptist heritage: "leaders of revolution against churches and social orders that were based upon principles and practiced ways of life which they believed to be hostile to the spirit of the gospel."

During the four years when he edited *Christian Frontiers* (1946-1949), he kept returning to the theme of the dangers of America's unstrained militarism. But the preeminent issue in its pages was the plight of the conscientious objectors of World War II. Strategically this was an issue his Southern Baptist readers could sympathize with, since freedom of conscience was a major tenet of the denomination.

> From the whipping posts of New England and the jails of Virginia, Baptists have affirmed the primacy of the individual conscience over the demands of the institutional church and totalitarian state. It was because they belonged to the heritage of freedom nurtured by the Baptist tradition that some fifty Southern Baptists followed the dictates of their consciences and registered as conscientious objectors. Southern Baptists trained them to be free, but the Brethren Service Commission paid the price of their freedom.[2]

The brave souls Finlator celebrated here were still being held in work camps and being denied their civil rights. Their own denomination seemed to have turned its back upon them, and their upkeep in the camps was being financed by a pacifist denomination, the Church of the Brethren. Finlator called for a general

---

[2]W. W. Finlator, "Free the Conscientious Objectors," *Christian Frontiers* 2 (June 1946): 181.

amnesty for them. In a June 1947 editorial he criticized the Southern Baptist Executive Committee for its "play-safe, do-nothing, no-comment attitude" manifest in its refusal to repay the Brethren $17,708 for the upkeep of these conscientious objectors and its failure to request President Truman to grant a general amnesty. Southern Baptists never did repay the Brethren for caring for their members, but Finlator had waded into waters he would never depart.

For the remainder of this chapter I will turn first to the beginnings of Finlator's concern for peace and follow that with a chronological account of his multifaceted peace ministry. With his denomination's record, Finlator had no reason to be oriented toward peace. Other than the witness of the traditional peace churches the peace cause was a mark of the Social Gospel during the 1930s when Finlator received his theological training. But the Social Gospel was not in vogue among Southern Baptists. As the world moved inexorably toward World War II, he did little to oppose America's entrance nor afterwards did he sound any alarm about the dropping of the atomic bomb.

While in his first pastorate at Pittsboro, before moving to Weldon in 1941, Finlator had stirred the wrath of the local branch of the American Legion by questioning the mobilization for war. Moreover, he expressed reservations about the propriety of flying the American flag in the church sanctuary. He also challenged the singing of "God Bless America" unless it was teamed with a song affirming God's like concern for all other nations. He had begun dispatching articles to the state Baptist paper. In the issue of 3 July 1940 he raised the question about patriotism and militarism in the light of Christian peacemaking. For the most part, though, his contributions contained not a word about the holocaust reducing Europe to rubble. Interviewed by the *Winston-Salem Journal,* on 8 September 1982, he expressed regrets that he had not protested more against war. He seemed more disturbed about what was happening at home. We are "fighting fascism abroad and tolerating it at home," was as far as he went in the *Recorder.*[3] Earlier, he had written in its pages,

---

[3]Finlator, "Pastors and Prejudice," *Biblical Recorder* 110 (15 March 1944): 7.

Now that we rightly guess that the victory of the Allies is not so remote perhaps as a nation we ought to apply that teaching to ourselves. Shall we not be on our guard against going all over the world crusading for our way of life, saying that everyone must think as we think, act as we act, live as we live?[4]

His strongest statement of the period analyzed the "Armageddon complex" within the national psyche.

God forbid that this Armageddon complex shall possess us when the representatives of the starving, bleeding, defeated peoples sit down with our leaders at the peace table. . . . From being a sort of biblical red herring within the Christian body it now becomes a misnomer whose consequences could gravely impair the efforts for a post-war world of decency. . . . Far nearer the truth is it to say that God *condemns* us to fight rather than commands us to fight. . . . We cannot say that we [Allies] are all white and you the Axis are all black. Alas, we know wherein we too have been guilty. . . . Rather then let soldiers of the Cross fight the good fight against economic isolationism and racial discrimination and inequality of wealth.[5]

Viewed today, many years after they were made, these scanty statements may seem ever so weak; only in the fiery heat of the war effort did they sound treasonous to some citizens. In the intervening years, prior to the Vietnam engagement, Finlator's commitment to nonviolence was preoccupied with the violence of segregation and the death penalty.

In the fall of 1964 Lyndon Johnson had been reelected president of the United States, campaigning as a moderate against the bellicose candidate Barry Goldwater. He had hardly counted the votes when he appealed for and got Senatorial approval for the Gulf of Tonkin Resolution that enabled him to escalate the fighting in Vietnam. It was against that backdrop that Finlator stood in the Pullen pulpit on 28 February 1965 and announced before

---

[4]Finlator, "I. O. U. Happiness," *Biblical Recorder* 109 (28 July 1943): 10.
[5]Finlator, "This Is Not Armageddon," *Biblical Recorder* 108 (17 June 1942): 10.

the morning prayer that he wished to read "a statement of concern."

> Let us in whatever reprieve may be granted us seek peace now
> and preserve it with intelligence, courage and humility. Let us
> assure the President of our support and prayers urging him to
> take steps immediately to separate our military from the con-
> flict. . . . Let us not be fearful of our national prestige or loss of
> face remembering that our true strength beyond our military
> might has been and still is our heritage of justice, peace, equality
> and freedom for all.

Finlator dispatched the Sunday morning appeal as an open telegram to President Johnson and was instantly marked as a leading "dove" in the South and among Baptists. His congregation
discovered they were to hear a great deal more on the subject and
that they would be obliged to share their pastor with the public.
Besides being in demand as a speaker against the war, he helped
organize the churches' resistance to the war concentrated in such
organizations as Clergy and Laity Concerned about Vietnam,
Negotiations Now, the North Carolina Committee Against the
Vietnam War, and the Interreligious Committee. With the latter
group he marched on the Pentagon in May. His congregation
would get used to seeing their pastor in strange places. He was
soon on the streets of the state capitol standing in silent vigil.
While some of his members stood aghast, others were in hostile
disagreement. His support came largely from outside the congregation and the Baptist denomination. Quakers—though by no
means all North Carolina Quakers—stood beside him. Speaking
of this in a sermon years later on 29 October 1978, he explained
"Why I Joined Them."

> In the third place I am identified with the Quakers. I am not
> actually a member of the Society of Friends. There is too much
> preacher in me to sit in long silence and wait for the spiritual
> consensus. But I am honored to be a part of that courageous, im-
> aginative and humane organization sponsored by the Quakers
> and known and honored around the world as the American
> Friends Service Committee. In a world where it is becoming in-
> creasingly difficult for oppressed people to redress their griev-

ances by non-violent means, especially since their oppressors do
not hesitate to resort to violence, the AFSC has stood foursquare
for "peaceful persuasion." I found them to be the few, the happy
few, the band of brothers who have a soul commitment to "let
truth speak to power," whether that power be governments, military establishments, corporations or culture. They come the
nearest of any people I know in carrying out literally the mandate of St. Paul that we are to overcome evil with good.

Many in his congregation supported Finlator's social witness
generally, even to defending the repetitiveness of his attacks on
the war. But within two years his emphasis was pressing their
tolerance. In 1966, he lectured on "The Dagger and the Cross" before the state Baptist Student Union stirring considerable controversy; he accompanied the American Friends Service
Committee to Washington on another antiwar protest; he gave a
speech at the Blue Ridge Assembly, "World Peace: A Spiritual
Imperative," which was widely reprinted; his Pullen sermon
against the war on 16 October was widely circulated, and in December he was a major figure in an ecumenical "Church Conference on Peace."

The year 1967 found him on 22 January preaching once again
on the subject. This sermon, "An American Tragedy," was inserted by Senator Wayne Morse into the *Congressional Record,*
and marked Finlator as one of America's most astute critics of the
Vietnam conflict.

In speaking today of the tragedy of our involvement in Vietnam I shall not talk, as on former occasions, about an unjust and
immoral war, or dwell on the bankruptcy of American foreign
policy so dramatized in Vietnam, or deplore the bombing of ci-
vilians, or describe the horror of napalm bombs or the shame of
the nauseating gas, or defoliation of the forests or the poisoning
of the rice fields. Indeed I shall talk about what the war is doing
to us as a nation and as a people. . . . I like to suggest that the
tragedy expresses itself in six ways: first, through Loss of Faith;
second, through Breach of Contract; third, in the Crisis of Credibility; fourth, through a Paralysis of Inner Enrichment; fifth, in
Default of Leadership; and sixth, through Schism of the Soul. . . .
What to do about it all? This is not the burden of my sermon to-

day. You already know how I feel. We went in unilaterally and we can come out unilaterally. Our interest there was self-created. We can uncreate it. But brethren, my heart's desire and prayer to God for America is that *they* might be saved! Saved from a tragedy of our own making.

The sermon was reprinted in four different journals. Letters of approval came from congressmen, judges, civic leaders at all levels, as well as from ordinary folk. Within his own congregation, however, even from among his most loyal supporters, there was considerable unrest. Typical are two letters written within the week following the sermon.

> While I cherish our traditionally "free pulpit" and share your dismay about our sad involvement in Vietnam, I am writing to ask you *please* to evaluate what you are doing when you continue your broadsides from the pulpit about Vietnam. . . . It is hard for me to see that further use of our pulpit to expound your point of view about Vietnam is constructive and responsible. *We know how you feel about it.* And if I, who am in general agreement with your position, feel alienated by your sermons on it, how much more so must those feel who are in violent disagreement with you?
>
> After church last Sunday, I asked several people just how they reacted to your sermon. While most of them agreed basically with your position, their comments included three observations: "Well, I surely didn't feel as if I had been to church." "It really gave me nothing spiritual to hold to." "Is Bill's main purpose to serve his own needs or ours? And isn't there some way for him to do both?" "Is it possible for Bill to make honest affirmation on any other basis than social justice?" I really hope that the answer to these last two questions is "yes."

Some members of the Pullen congregation were getting fed up with their pastor's heavy peace emphasis. How much of this negative reaction pertained to Finlator's homiletic style rather than his position at odds with public opinion is hard to tell. "Vietnam seemed to upset the congregation, and the public, more than anything else I had done up to that moment," Finlator commented in retrospect. "It sounded like betrayal or treason. The people had sons in service. North Carolina State University of course, like

most institutions, was more or less involved in the war effort. The
congregation was just not up to dealing with a pastor who stood
in open defiance against his nation at war. And, I hasten to add,
I must have bored in too heavily upon them, preaching too many
sermons on the subject. They had a right to squirm."

Public opposition came to a head with the treatment accorded
him by the state Baptist convention meeting in Asheville in November 1967 when he submitted a resolution against the war. He
was treated so rudely by the official body and ridiculed by some
of the press that his congregation became even more embarrassed by their pastor. Finlator recalled some of the reaction.

> I remember the church treasurer who was also on the Board
> of Deacons wrote a letter to me submitting his resignation in pro-
> test. This came after the debacle at the Convention. I think he
> was thoroughly put out with me at that moment, probably out-
> raged. He had two sons who may have been headed for service.
> Then there were those letters from the congregation. Whether
> this was a concerted venture or whether it was spontaneous I don't
> know but they came pretty close together, all strongly protesting
> my involvement in the war protest. And then there was a very
> excellent man, once the Chairman of the Board and now a chan-
> cellor of a university system in another state, who told me in love
> and anger that Sunday after Sunday somewhere along the con-
> gregation knew that Vietnam would be appearing here, there or
> yonder. When it came they finally relaxed, well here it is and now
> it's passed!

In the face of this growing hostility, Finlator's own faith in his
peace witness wavered; perhaps he was wrong, or was moving too
fast. Accordingly, he used the occasion of his annual Christmas
letter to the congregation (1967) to announce a retreat.

> I write this personal message voluntarily to express deepest
> regret for the distress and anguish I have brought to you during
> the past two years with regard to the involvement of our nation
> in Vietnam. Most of you have not shared my views and all of you
> have been patient and long-suffering. I feel that in the warmth
> and depth of my convictions I have taken advantage of your
> kindness, and your silence, in sermons and articles and direct ac-
> tion. I am aware that I have gone too far and presumed too long

upon your forbearance and I want so much to find the right word and do the right thing to make what amends I can.

For this reason I am this week severing my relationship with the Raleigh Peace Vigil and shall no more on Wednesdays stand with the group in silent protest in front of the Post Office. . . .

Furthermore as I review my preaching I must acknowledge that all too frequently, perhaps repetitiously, the matter of Vietnam has been in my sermons. And of course I am embarrassed over the unfortunate publicity [about his praise of the students' picketing]. Thus it is my pledged intent that future statements within, and activities beyond, our church and community, without compromising the witness one feels he has to make, indicate a deference to your feeling and honor our relationship with one another here at Pullen. I am sorry that it is at the Christmas season I write you these words. Another time might have been much more appropriate.

Since it left the impression that the freedom of the pulpit was in jeopardy and that their pastor was weak-kneed, it was misinterpreted and in some ways the letter backfired, accomplishing not at all what the writer had intended. "Many members took it as my way of saying subtly that I had been intimidated by the congregation," Finlator recalls. "Others took it as unnecessarily airing my own misgivings. Still others were grieviously hurt and expressed strong guilt that I was obliged to make public such a feeling. In any case, it had the opposite effect intended; it tended to focus more acutely on the problem rather than to relieve matters." Finlator lived to regret the letter, because it bears witness to the speculation that he was in cowardice reining in his prophetic ministry. "I wish I had not written it," he says now, "though I was under a great deal of pressure at the time. The pressure may have been more imaginary than real. I still regret that letter and I think it was a mistake."

Fortunately for the nation's health and the work of peace forces in America, Finlator did not remain silent or inactive very long. The lesson for Finlator was to be more fully conscious of how deeply ingrained the war mentality was even among his many "liberal" friends. "I was beginning to see the raw militarism and imperialism of my country," he says. In the years 1968 and 1969 he actually accelerated his campaign against the war—hammering on the doors of government officials, flooding the press with statements and petitioning church councils. He even added one more segment of the populace to his list: organized labor. By this time Finlator was fully involved with labor and was heartily accepted by its leadership. Many labor leaders also endorsed the Vietnam war. After persistent pleas that they dissociate themselves from the government policy, he finally resorted to an open letter to the national office, dated 11 October 1969. George Meany, national president of the AFL-CIO, replied on 15 October, begging to disagree. Finlator answered Meany on 28 October.

> I am grateful that you found time to respond personally to my letter of concern regarding the support of the AFL-CIO of the policy of the Administration in Vietnam. I must remind you, however, that in my judgement, organized labor has through its almost doctrinaire support of the Administration forfeited much of the sympathy of former friends. . . . These voices just cannot be ignored and there seems to be a consensus among them with regard to what I have written you. I do wish to assure you, however, of my belief in and deep sympathy for the cause of organized labor.

Subsequent shifts in "hard hat" sentiment against Vietnam received some applause and support from Finlator.

With his own household, the Baptists, he was not so successful. In 1969, as in previous years, his three resolutions—one against the war, one against the nation's militarism, one in defense of conscientious objectors—placed before both state and national bodies of Baptists had difficulty even reaching the floor. A not quite sympathetic account was filed by a columnist for the *Biblical Recorder*.

> Few persons seem as capable of stirring the emotions of North Carolina Baptists as W. W. Finlator. He is a liberal as far as social action is concerned and is prone to ply his views from the podium whenever the Baptist State Convention or Southern Baptist Convention is in annual session. He must earnestly believe in that adage about trying and trying again, because as sure as the convention meets, you can be sure Bill will be on the platform. Such

was the case last week in Fayetteville. When resolutions time came there was Bill ready to step to the microphone. This time it was "resolution on restitution." Later he was back with one on amnesty for imprisoned or exiled conscientious objectors to military service. He also got in on the discussion on the resolution concerning treatment of prisoners of war. He was asked to come to the platform to point where the change was to be made. As he walked to the stage, one far western North Carolina pastor, in a magnanimous gesture of Christian charity, said to him as he walked past, "I hope you fall in the orchestra pit."[6]

During 1969 the antiwar movement originated plans for a moratorium day. On the first scheduled day, 15 October, Finlator was the featured speaker for massive rallies on three different campuses, at Meredith College, Chapel Hill and on Salem Square in Winston-Salem.

By 1970 he finally succeeded in getting his antiwar resolution to the floor of the Baptist convention, but it was so watered down by the committee, chaired by a Dr. Bland, that processed it, that it was known among his friends as the "bland" resolution. Southern Baptists remained at this late date one of the few Protestant denominations not to disown the war. Finlator would not let them off the hook. In 1971 and 1972 he introduced resolutions to force Baptists to decide, first in St. Louis, calling for the demilitarization of the United States, and then in Philadelphia, calling once again for withdrawal. In his 1971 resolution, Finlator called America to beat its swords into implements to feed the hungry.

> Whereas: The war in Indo China, undeclared and longest in our history, with a tonnage of bombs dropped alone upon Vietnam in excess of the total tonnage dropped by the Allies over all of Europe in World War II, haunts and grinds the conscience of America. And, despite the manifest futility of the war, the destruction and atrocities visited, the disillusionment and cynicism of our servicemen abroad and the disruption and despair of our citizens at home, our leaders cry peace, peace, when there is no peace.
>
> Now therefore be it resolved that

---

[6]Toby Druin (weekly column), *Biblical Recorder* 135 (22 November 1969): 22.

1) The Southern Baptist Convention call upon the President of the United States to announce forthwith a day not later than July 1, 1972, by which time all American military power shall be completely withdrawn.

2) That the federal government commit itself immediately to a massive relocation of the national resources of our country to the end that the eighty billions of dollars earmarked each year for the Pentagon shall be drastically reduced and diverted to the claimant and unmet domestic need of the country.

His petition went unheeded.

On the political front in 1972, in addition to standing vigil at the White House in protest against President Nixon's escalation of the bombing raids, he added his weight to the impeachment movement against Nixon. However, Finlator received more flak from his criticism of Billy Graham's stance on the war than about his opposition to Nixon. In his public letter Finlator argued that Dr. Graham

has long been a Cold War warrior accepting the premise that the world is divided between the good and the evil, the free and the slave, the capitalist and the communist, and this devil's theory is supported by the vast military build-up of our nation and intervention into the affairs of other nations. This justifies the massive preparation for Armageddon against international communism. From the outset he has been a hawk with regard to our involvement in Vietnam, giving spiritual sanction to a cause that is now universally repudiated.[7]

Amnesty became Finlator's major theme for the years 1973 and 1974, especially as President Ford's pardon of Richard Nixon accompanied his indifference to the plight of the young persons victimized by their antiwar beliefs. In a 1973 article Finlator offered "A Plea for Amnesty."

In my judgement there are occasions in history when no policy other than amnesty is effective. Our President has traveled to China and to Russia and in effect said to the leaders of these

---

[7]Finlator, "I'll Skip Billy Graham," *Churchman* (October 1973): 3.

erstwhile enemy nations: "Let bygones be bygones and in the interest of peace and friendship let's just forget on both sides. . . ."

You wonder if the President can extend amnesty to our sworn enemies of yesterday why he feels so vindictive and obdurate toward his fellow Americans. The President is committed to bringing us all together again and those thousands upon thousands of war resisters have families and friends and sympathizers by the hundreds of thousands throughout the land.

Our nation has a grievance against these war resisters for what it regards as desertion in an hour of crisis. On the other hand the war resisters have a grievance against the nation for forcing them into an intolerable position regarding their conscience. Instead of asking for forgiveness they think in terms of *granting* forgiveness. Neither side feels guilt from wrongdoing and therefore repentance and contrition, reparation, restoration, exacting of penalties, etc. are beside the point. Your reference to lack of courage seems unfortunate, since many of these resisters have gone willingly to Federal jail out of convictions of conscience, the safeguarding of which is a dear, dear Baptist tenet. The only way out of this impasse is simply forgetting, or amnesia, on both sides.[8]

Using his influence in the American Civil Liberties Union, Finlator tried to bring pressure on the president to provide something other than the Clemency Board with its recriminatory provisos for draft resisters and deserters. He drafted the ACLU's rejection of the offer of clemency.

The proposal shows that President Ford and his advisors have learned nothing about a tragic, illegal and shameful war, and are willing to use the plight of hundreds of thousands of young men to assert the legitimacy of our involvement in Southeast Asia. It imposes upon the evaders and deserters two years of what really amounts to compulsory labor, the taking of loyalty oaths and the acceptance of discharges under punitive and stigmatizing circumstances.

Even with the negotiated settlement of the war in the spring of 1975, Finlator could not dismiss the affair with a sigh of relief.

---

[8]Finlator, "A Plea for Amnesty," *Churchman* (April 1973): 5.

In a sermon to his congregation on 4 May he summarized the continuing consequences.

> We are an anguished people, in direct need of justice, compassion and humility, who through 25 years of tragic and shameless involvement in Southeast Asia have neither done justice, nor loved mercy, nor walked humbly with God or man.
>
> In disregarding our Constitution, in violating the Charter of the United Nations, in bypassing the provisions of the Geneva Accords, in contravening the prohibitions of the SEATO, in propagating lies and myths and self-deceptions at home and abroad, we have become purveyors of injustice and international outlawry.
>
> In devastating a long-plagued peasant land and people, in defoliating forests, poisoning fields and slaughtering cattle, in making million upon millions homeless, refugees and orphaned, in total and wanton destruction of a culture in order to win hearts and minds, and in the sacrifice of American youth and the diversion of resources and energies from our own cities and land and people, we have not loved mercy. We have become strangers to compassion.[9]

When Jimmy Carter, a Southern Baptist, was elected President, Finlator saw a unique opportunity. Twice, in 1977 and in 1980, he addressed public letters to President Carter appealing to his Baptist heritage, as is evident in the first letter. "The church, the local Baptist church in Plains, has shaped your character, informed your conscience and structured your integrity. For this we thank God." In both letters he stressed the qualities necessary to salvage America from a false messianic militarism. The 1980 letter read, in part, "Your Baptist faith is about to be put to the greatest test. . . . Please let me, therefore, as Baptist to Baptist, urge you to resist the terrific temptation to draw the mantle of religion over the actions of our government and to equate our foreign policy with the will of God." Finlator was disappointed that the President never acknowledged his appeal. Even when he visited the Carter White House he was never able to pursue the subject.

---

[9]Finlator, "A Short Sermon," *U.S. Farm News* (July 1975).

Finlator was not to be dissuaded or discouraged though. In the years 1979 and 1980 he was back before the state and Southern Baptist Conventions introducing resolutions. One asking for backing of the Salt II Treaty and the other against the reinstitution of the military draft. In the spring of 1980, as the warmindedness of the Reagan administration mounted, marked by the training on American soil of troops from Central America, Finlator protested the policy in Washington and at the gates of Ft. Bragg, where many Central American troops were encamped. "I have," he told the press,

> come to call judgment upon the administration, and upon our President, for the cynical decision to continue, and to expand, military assistance to one of the most consistently repressive and murderous governments on earth in face of documented evidence, known internally, that the security forces of El Salvador are wantonly stripping their people of every last vestige of human rights and in a systematic orgy are brutalizing, torturing and killing them, thousands upon thousands. . . . And, finally, I have come to plead with all Americans to take alarm that another Vietnam, with all its tragedy and futility, is, and has been, in the making which, in addition to multiplying death and destruction in El Salvador and further alienating us from the family of nations will rend the fabric of our own society and force us to violate our cherished commitments to justice, equity, humanity, peace and freedom.

This announcement provoked the usual barrage of unfavorable mail. One letter read, "When I read this article it made me sick at my stomach. Just knowing there are characters such as yourself in this country, accepting our freedom and stabbing our country in the back at the same time."

In the fall of 1982 Finlator produced another public letter endorsing the concept of the nuclear-free zone.

> I suggest and urge as a "modest proposal" that the city of Raleigh is a nuclear free zone. Such a declaration would in effect quietly announce to the U.S., Russia and the world that our community has, on our own and with no preconditions, opted out of the nuclear madness . . . that we are not waiting for our government to negotiate a mutually verifiable agreement but are tak-

ing matters into our own hands and telling our government that our turf here is off limits to the production, design, testing, deployment, and use of nuclear weapons. We are renouncing our right, whatever that is, to be defended, and we are asking to be taken off the target lists of any government that produces nuclear weapons.[10]

At Campbell College in the spring of 1983 he once again challenged the nation's inordinate military spending, in a debate with a general. The Campbell *Prospect* for May reported his reworking of a parable of Jesus.

> A certain rich nation had a massive gross national product. This was expressed in a great proliferation of weaponry. And the nation began to say to itself: "What shall I do with all this megatonnage? I have no place to keep my ships. I have no airfields here at home to care for this growth of airplanes. I have no silos to take care of my MX missiles. I know what I will do. I will build larger ports. I will convert my Polaris and Poseidon submarines. I will do away with my long-range missiles and I'll put them there. I will make my navy so great they everybody will be scared, and then I'll lean back and say, America, you are now secure with all this nuclear fission. Eat, drink, and enjoy your consumerism." And the Lord said, "Thou fool, this night thy soul shall be required of thee."[11]

At this time Finlator was in his second year of retirement but he devoted himself more freely to combatting the current administration's war threats and military policy. And he now had more time to give to the other main branch of his crusade against violence, his opposition to capital punishment and the prison system.

When he had become the pastor of Pullen he had made repeal of the death penalty and prison reform priorities of his ministry. Perhaps the location of North Carolina's penitentiary within a block of Pullen haunted him. Along with playwright Paul Green

---

[10]Finlator, Letter to the Editor, *News and Observer* (Raleigh NC), 2 December 1982, 8.

[11]Finlator, "Debate on Nuclear Weapons," *Campbell University Prospect* (May 1983): 22.

and lawyer Marion Wright he founded an organization, North Carolinians against the Death Penalty. Pullen hosted the organizational meeting and Finlator was elected to the governing board in 1967. The three remained steadfastly devoted to this cause over the years. In the eulogy he delivered at Paul Green's funeral in 1981, Finlator reminisced about Green's dedication to the cause.

> He had a profound and simple love for human beings. He was against anything that prevented each person from reaching his or her potential—whether it be race, sex, religion or economic status. This led him to oppose capital punishment. He felt that capital punishment was saying to a person that we give up on you, there is no possibility of redemption for you. I recall he would come to Raleigh, visit the prison, and talk hour on hour with the men on death row, understanding their stories and how they got there. He was determined that society would not dehumanize these people.

When Finlator himself was awarded the North Carolina Civil Liberties Union award in 1980, Marion Wright rendered the tribute: "A true humanist, Finlator believes that no state should put a man to death for—of all things—putting a man to death, and that only folly or a form of insanity should cause a state to believe that men are reformed by shutting them off for some years from all humanizing influences."

In 1983, when the state legalized the penalty of death by lethal injection, Finlator—who for many years as legislative chairman for the state Civil Liberties Union had kept that organization pressuring the state to rid itself of the death penalty—represented its opposition on 31 May. "I think the word 'humane' is intriguing," he said. "There is not a humane way to kill someone. That's a euphemism that doesn't hold water. It was made to make capital punishment more palatable. The only way to make it more humane is to abolish it." The earliest position paper of the North Carolina Civil Liberties Union on capital punishment had been prepared by Finlator; he read it before the North Carolina House Judiciary Committee on 11 March 1965.

I am grateful for the privilege of joining other concerned citizens of our state in urging the complete and final abolition of
capital punishment by this session of the General Assembly. The
compelling logic for the removal of this vestige of medieval bar-
barity and punitive sterility is by now well known and, I trust,
convincing to our minds and consciences. . . . We are asking of
you gentlemen no radical action. The people of North Carolina,
the conscience of our commonwealth, have already abolished
capital punishment. We simply ask that you take official cogni-
zance of this. We ask you only to give it a prompt and decent burial. Let no one henceforth be tempted to inject into its corpse the
hypodermic of dark hope nor by any sorcery or incantation seek
its macabre resurrection. Let us end this spiritual damage on all
society.

Within the decade the U.S. Supreme Court outlawed capital
punishment as then practiced. Finlator appeared again before the
legislature's Judiciary Committee on 29 October 1976.

For the first time in its history North Carolina has no death
penalty and no death row and, as Senator Ervin would say, the
heavens have not fallen! Nobody has reported an increase in
homicides or a breakdown in law enforcement yet North Carolinians live, move and have their being today without capital
punishment on the statutes.

Any victory celebration was premature as Finlator had to appear before the same committee on 23 February 1981. He be-
moaned the moment

when the mood of the nation has moved to the right, a time when
liberty and justice for all has fewer friends and growing opposition among the powerful and influential in Washington, a time
when the Bill of Rights becomes secondary. . . . [But] the Civil
Liberties Union is determined in its opposition to cruel and unusual punishment when this means in an enlightened age bar-
barous treatment of prisoners and the administration of the death
penalty.

Finlator had learned too well that the price of liberty and social
progress is eternal vigilance. In 1974 he had given his "Declaration of Conscience" at a major rally in Raleigh protesting the

death penalty; within five years he was obliged to confess defeat. "We are met," he told the press,

> to express shock and repugnance for the return to our nation of state-imposed death penalty which we view as legalized murder. We are saddened that after a period when the conscience and consensus of America seemed to be moving toward a total disavowal of capital punishment we are now witnessing a regression to this barbarous and inhuman relic which has been discredited and rejected in other nations and cultures today. We remember with anguish the people on death row. We call upon our religious leaders, our political leaders and all people of good will to pledge that the death penalty shall henceforth and forever be repudiated in North Carolina.

Parallel with his annual siege of the legislative halls Finlator was also pleading with his fellow Baptists. In the fall of 1962 he managed to get the issue before the state Baptist Convention. The stage was set for a classic confrontation, between a diehard, Judge Johnson J. Hayes, and a liberal, Irving Carlyle, both prominent Baptist jurists. When the former harangued the crowd to a screaming endorsement of the death penalty, Finlator's resolution was drowned in a torrent of emotion. Finlator was deeply saddened by this vindictive display within his own spiritual household. On 1 November, his letter appeared in the *Biblical Recorder*.

> One of the best arguments for the abolition of capital punishment insured its defeat at the recent convention. This was the high voltage attack by Judge Hayes upon the recommendation of the Christian Life Committee for abolition in North Carolina. Were this supreme penalty outlawed, never again could a man unleash before a church assembly, or elsewhere, such an orgy of fear and vindictiveness and obscurantism. Never again would faces visibly harden when crimes already familiar to everyone were depicted so fiendishly and luridly by a distinguished judge who chose to return to duty of solicitorship and convert a Baptist Convention into a criminal court. Never again could Pandora's box of hatred and recrimination be opened upon a people who had been prepared to face with calmness and rationality an issue that confronts Christian conscience with increasing urgency.

Finlator would not give up on his fellow Baptists. Both before his own congregation and before Baptist groups at large he continued his pleading. Baptist students at Wake Forest University, after hearing his argument before them in February 1968, formed a group that spearheaded a banning resolution for the fall state convention. This time it passed, though in a weakened version.

Lieutenant Governor James Hunt, who had been a member of Pullen when a student at the state university, was a candidate for governor in 1976. Since Finlator had been Hunt's pastor he tried, under an ad hoc committee for repeal of the death penalty, to persuade Hunt to include this plank in his platform. Hunt refused and in the ensuing years of his successful office-holding remained adamant, becoming in 1984 the first North Carolina governor in two decades to preside over an execution.

Finlator also challenged Billy Graham on his hardline stance. In a Pullen church bulletin of 1973, given wide press coverage, he revealed that "Dr. Graham has long been a supporter of capital punishment which is part of his hard-nosed and repressive attitude in dealing with crime." In another letter in 1973 Finlator questioned "Graham's Plan."

> It is shocking to read. Billy Graham has advocated the castration of convicted rapists as a means of deterrence. . . . I shudder at the consequences of the plan. I am aware of his biblical literalism but cannot but wonder at the strict construction he seems to be putting on Jesus' words: "If thine eye offend thee pluck it out." . . . Perhaps his advocacy of maiming is not so shocking, however, when we remember that in the same press conference he reiterated his support for the return of capital punishment. . . . His words, which carry such massive weight, reflect and reinforce the wave of oppression and vindictiveness sweeping over us. I am saddened and frightened by them. He speaks so often of judgement and retribution.[12]

Finlator viewed the death penalty within the larger context of how society defines "crime," whom it chooses to prosecute and imprison, and how incarceration is managed. Accordingly, he ap-

---

[12]Finlator, "Graham's Plan," *Biblical Recorder* (7 April 1973): 12.

pealed to North Carolinians Against the Death Penalty "to broaden our objectives to include the entire area of prison reform." In the report he composed for the organization's gathering in High Point on 15 September 1970, he reasoned,

> In urging that we enlarge our concern, the committee would cite certain instances, under our present system, of homicides within the prison, of attempted escapees being shot down, of the horror of "death row," and of the living death within the walls of the prison of those who have escaped the death chamber. We can save a life from execution only to lose it in the murky cells of human degradation. We therefore must move from abolition to reform. . . . We must also move to the administration of criminal justice. We cannot effectively achieve reformation of the prison system and rehabilitation of a prisoner, even with such welcomed changes as newer buildings, more humane and better paid administrators and custodians, conjugal visits, work and educational opportunities, etc. until we are willing to reform, perhaps revolutionize, the entire judicial process that apprehends, tries, convicts, and sentences the prisoner.

Soon thereafter Finlator was privileged to be appointed to a position of some influence in these matters. He became chairman of the North Carolina Advisory Committee on Civil Rights. From this platform he staged an open hearing on the prison system on 24-25 May 1974.

Finlator's untiring crusade had been fueled by his personal compassion for prisoners themselves. Very early he had risked his own career in the South by cosigning with Martin Luther King, Jr., Clarence Jordan, and James McBride Dabbs, 9 October 1961, a petition to President Kennedy to have Carl Braden released from jail. (He had been charged with contempt by the House Un-American Activities Committee.) That was the first instance of his public identification with key prisoners. In 1962, he pled for Junius Scales; in November 1963 he visited the Williamston jail where fifteen Northern preachers, including Harvey Cox, were being held; he came to King's side in his repeated imprisonments; he tried to prevent Muhammad Ali from being imprisoned as a conscientious objector; in 1970 he marched with Coretta King and others protesting the presence of a eighteen-year-old girl, Marie Hill, on death row. He visited Ms. Hill in Central Prison, carrying her a guitar. When Dr. Jim Grant, one of the Charlotte Three prisoners he befriended, was moved to Raleigh, he took him books to read. Correspondence with Dr. Grant and hundreds of other prisoners fills Finlator's files.

Even before world attention focused on the plight of the Wilmington Ten, Finlator was present at a hearing on their behalf on 1 September 1974; he helped gather the names of one hundred Southern clergymen to urge Governor Hunt to pardon them; he chaired the Advisory Committee when the resolution passed appealing to the U.S. Justice Department to review their case; and on 29 September 1976 he intervened on behalf of Ben Chavis, who though on a release-study program at Duke Divinity School still was refused pardon by Governor Hunt. On 25 March 1977, he addressed a letter to President Carter, conveying to him

> appreciation and encouragement for the position of your administration regarding safeguarding of human rights around the world. . . . Since justice, like charity, begins at home, we welcome and support the concern of your administration for such cases as the Wilmington Ten and the Charlotte Three. The involvement of your administration in these trials will serve to remove the vulnerability of our nation to the charge, "Physician, heal thyself," from abroad and at the same time bring hope to us that the dark clouds of doubt and uncertainty shall be lifted from our State.

These expressions of Finlator's passion for peace graphically illustrate his paradoxical role within Southern religious culture. Though not a pacifist, he was too radical for most Baptists and Southerners but not radical enough for his friends Clarence Jordan and Daniel Berrigan. On the Vietnam war he was too radical for many members of his congregation and for most Baptists, radical enough to the FBI to warrant its continuing surveillance of his activities, but not radical enough for the pro-Hanoi antiwar element. On prison reform and the decriminalization of victimless crimes he was too radical for most of the public and for many within the Civil Liberties Union but not radical enough for the "born-again" Charles Colson, President Nixon's White House lawyer, who after serving time in prison for his Watergate crimes was now crusading for the release of all captives and the abolition of prisons. The varying degrees of "peacefulness" are reflected in Finlator's own personal position. While he manifested a moderate stance, he differed from many conservative Christians who conceptualized "the peace of Christ" either as a personal internalized salvation or as realizable on earth only in an apocalyptic future. He understood Christ to have instituted a realistic peace-making here and now.

Chapter Six

SEPARATING CHURCH AND STATE

IN AMERICA, THE CONCEPT of separation of church and state received its major impetus when Roger Williams was banished from Massachusetts in 1635 and founded the settlement called Providence, designed, as he said, "to be a shelter for persons distressed in conscience." Williams formulated the doctrine of the neutral state in his famous "ship of state" analogy.

> There goes many a ship to sea, with many hundred souls in one ship, whose weal and woe is common, and is a true picture of a commonwealth. . . . It hath fallen out sometimes, that both papists and protestants, Jews and Turks, may be embarked in one ship: upon which supposal I affirm, that all the liberty of conscience, that ever I pleaded for, turns upon these two hinges—that none be forced to come to the ship's prayers or worship, nor compelled from their own particular prayers or worship, if they practice any.

Sunday after Sunday, for the twenty-six years he preached in the Pullen pulpit, Finlator faced the spirit of Roger Williams, enshrined in a stained glass window. Williams had emerged as something of a Baptist saint, although he had remained a Baptist for only a short time after establishing the first Baptist church in America, in Providence, Rhode Island. He happened onto this honored place in the Pullen sanctuary not because he was generally honored among contemporary Southern Baptists but because the pastor prior to Finlator, Dr. E. McNeil Poteat, had held Williams in high esteem. Finlator pressed this adoration to the point of being viewed by many as Roger Williams *redivivus*.

For Finlator the principle in its most thoroughgoing application implies "freedom *from* religion" as well as "freedom of religion"; those with no religion must be as protected as those professing religion. Whenever Finlator cited the Founding Fathers, he made sure not to omit reference to atheists. In his 1977 letter to President Carter, reminding him of his Baptist affiliation, he wrote: "We must remember that this nation, in its neutrality toward religion, has housed great souls such as the Paines, the Franklins, the Jeffersons, and of course Emerson, Thoreau, Whitman and Robert Ingersoll." Thus the state itself, in all its governing functions and agencies and officials, cannot favor religion as such. For Finlator this meant neither favoring any particular religion or taking unto itself any religious prerogative. The "wall of separation" allows for neither favoring religion nor penalizing religion.

Finlator was well aware that he was in deep controversial waters with the best Constitutional authorities in America. But he derived his guidance from his Baptist doctrine, calling the principle "a Baptist distinctive." "Basically a Baptist is a person who stands for religious freedom" he said in a 1981 speech in Chapel Hill. "This freedom carries a very strong emphasis on freedom from religion as well. We have to respect the right of people to be agnostic, atheist, skeptics, antireligious, humanists, secularists and what not. If you don't honor them, then you don't honor religious freedom." More than thirty years earlier, in an editorial for *Christian Frontiers* in January 1948, he had espoused the same view. In the interval he had urged this interpretation on his Baptist peers with characteristic effrontery. He brought it to the floor of their conventions almost yearly, notably in 1963, 1969, 1971, 1972, 1974, 1978, 1979, 1980, and 1981. The principle of his resolution hardly changed; he called for support of "the doctrine of separation of church and state with its restraint upon government either to inhibit or to help the church in its worship and vocation and its restraint upon the church to use the state in furtherance of its worship and vocation."

What made Finlator's interpretation more radical than the average Baptist's was his insistence on the "secular state" aspect. In a sermon on 21 March 1963, he sounded his basic note: "To be Baptist with our history is to witness to the espousal of a free church in a secular state." Introducing his resolution to the 1980 Baptist State Convention, he said, "I reject the myth of a Christian nation, as do all true Baptists." His resolution asked the delegates to "reaffirm its unswerving commitment to the historic Baptist principle of church and state, so dearly purchased by our forebears, and its rejection therefore of the myth of a Christian nation, the equating or identifying of the Christian faith with any cause or ideology whether political, economic or religious, and the prescribed worship and devotion in institutions and agencies of government." In a 1974 sermon, "People Also Must Have Freedom from Religion," he explained the social value of such a position.

> Religion in America has all too few critics from the inside: when this is so it is inevitable that critics from the outside shall rise and have their day. Mrs. O'Hair [the secularist who perennially assailed the tendency toward "Christianization"] in a sense is a nemesis to the silencing by the church of the prophetic voices within.

The term "secular state" became the code word associated with Finlator's interpretation of the historic Roger Williams theory. As early as 21 March 1963 he had composed for discussion by the Baptist Public Affairs Committee a position paper against the North Carolina constitution that disqualified an unbeliever for office.

But to be Baptists in a state where we have wielded such vast influence, to be Baptists with our history of and witness to the espousal of a free church in a secular state, and to have enacted and retained such a statute in the supreme law of the land is past comprehension! Unless it is true that we really don't believe in church-state separation except up to a point. Unless it really is true that we never have been willing to entrust our earthly security to a religiously neutral state. Unless on the other hand we have been willing to compromise our high sounding phrases of religious liberty and the rights of conscience so far as to sacrifice or intimidate a few free thinkers, skeptics and atheists!

Beyond reminding Baptists of their historic principle and their share in getting it into the U.S. Constitution, he set himself up as the watchdog of the principle in the public arena. He alerted governing officials of any violations he saw, he lobbied the legislature for laws strengthening the wall of separation, cheered the Supreme Court when it decided in favor of strict division. In his ardor he sometimes found violations in the unlikeliest places. He challenged the state planetarium for its "Christmas star" show, the state legislature for its Good Friday services, the state highway department for its state map containing a "motorist's prayer," state supplements to religious colleges from tax monies, prayer in the public schools, the tax-exempt status of church property, legislation to enforce church-sponsored moral codes (such as laws prohibiting obscenity, alcohol consumption, and abortion), the so-called "Christian Amendment" to the U.S. Constitution, and President Reagan for his proclamation of the Year of the Bible. With such a varied list of adversaries, firmly entrenched in what they considered to be the American way, Finlator found himself constantly debating the precise parameters of the principle of separation.

His main foes were those Christian bodies that did not share the principle and those patriotic Americans who were altogether persuaded that this nation was established as a religious, if not a Christian, nation. Contrary to Finlator, who held that the Founding Fathers deliberately built in safeguards against religion, these persons contended that many of the Founders were religious—if not Christian, at least deists—and did not intend so strict a separation. Dr. Charles Lowry, formerly of the Washington Cathedral, argued this position with Finlator in a published debate.

> As a Christian and an American I am concerned with the antithesis of beliefs you set up and with your interpretation of historic American church-state doctrine. . . . But they [Founding Fathers] did emphasize religion and its public importance. The idea of proscribing public prayer and public recognition of God and His sovereignty would have horrified the men who made America. . . . Finally, there is surely no doubt that the Old Testament, specifically, and the New Testament, by implication, see nations and peoples as under God and responsible to Him. It is our religious heritage of the Bible which raises the issue of a true Church-State position and will not let it rest from the point of view of continuing decision and witness. Do you agree with this or are you prepared to break up with the central Biblical view of God and the nation-state?[1]

Finlator answered at length.

> I hope no one will ever call this nation or any other nation Christian. When I regard what nations seem to think they must do, and that includes such things as seeking not first the Kingdom of God but seeking their own self-interests, not believing in the power of the Spirit but the power of the Pentagon, not blessing our enemies and praying for those who do us wrong but punishing and excluding them, etc. All that I know of as a Christian and all that I see that my country seems to feel it must do and does do, some of which is true of other nations also, I can never say that this country is, or has been, or ever will be a "Christian" nation, but it has been and always will be, I trust, a nation where Christians can practice and evangelize without interference of government.[2]

Finlator found his strongest ally in the American Civil Liberties Union. Its North Carolina branch was organized at a meet-

---

[1]Charles Lowry, "Two Eminent Preachers Engage in Debate," *Sandhills Citizen* (Aberdeen NC), 10 December 1980, 2.

[2]W. W. Finlator, "Two Eminent Preachers Engage in Debate," *Sandhills Citizen* (Aberdeen NC), 10 December 1980, 2.

ing in the Pullen Church in 1965 and Finlator remained chairman
of its legislative committee for nearly two decades. He ultimately
became vice-chairman of the National Board. He considered the
ACLU to be as necessary to the preservation of civil liberties as
Baptists were to the preservation of the separation of church and
state. Appearing before a hearing of the constitution convention
committee on 29 May 1969, he declared, "As to the Bill of Rights
I have come to regard it as almost as sacrosanct as far as our government is concerned as is the Sermon on the Mount to the
churches. I am not sure that we could get such a Bill of Rights today." Finlator found in the Bill of Rights the legal authority for
his Baptist doctrine. Addressing the U.S. Senate Judiciary Committee on 28 April 1983, concerning the Hatfield bill designed to
permit religious groups to meet in public schools, Finlator, while
identifying himself as an official representative of the ACLU,
added that "I am pleased to observe in passing that my Baptist
heritage of free conscience, free speech and assembly, uncoerced
faith and practice, and church-state separation reinforce my
commitment to those same principles in which the ACLU lives
and moves and has its being."

Even so, the radical zeal with which he pursued Baptist doctrine encountered powerful elements within the ACLU that did
not wish to push the interpretation as far as Finlator did. Nat
Hentoff, also a member of the ACLU national board, attacked
Finlator in the *Village Voice*. While admiring the oratorical skills
of this Southern preacher, he could not accept what he considered
an extreme position. He praised the delivery of a Finlator speech
at a recent ACLU board meeting.

> I wish all of you could hear Bill Finlator preach. I've not heard
> such compelling a capella music since I was one of James Mi-
> chael Curley's announcers on a Boston radio station long ago. Like
> Curley, Reverend Finlator needs no text, for the spirit never fails
> him. He seldom raises his voice, being somewhat like the early
> Miles Davis in this respect; but even Miles, sinuous as he still is,
> has something to learn about dynamics from Bill Finlator.[3]

---

[3]Nat Hentoff, "Dread Speech Even the ACLU Will Not Protect," *Village Voice*,
24 May 1983, 8.

But on the content of Finlator's speech, defending the ACLU policy of opposing *all* religious activities of any group on public school property, Hentoff took strong exception.

> But for God's sake, the First Amendment does also include the guarantee of Free Exercise of Religion. Sure, there's tension between it and the Establishment Clause, but if you give one too much weight, it will swallow the other. Yet, the ACLU is so terrified that someone will trick Government into favoring a religion on school premises that it is squeezing the life out of the Free Exercise Clause. In this context, the ACLU is not neutral but actively hostile to religion. . . . If Bill Finlator is in good voice, the ACLU will continue to treat *all* expressions of religious speech in the public schools as if they were felons.[4]

The charge brought by Nat Hentoff from within the highest circles of the ACLU—hostility toward religion—was precisely the charge lodged against Finlator by the religious conservatives, within both the Southern Baptist fold and the Moral Majority. They contended, "Finlator is destroying religion to preserve a principle." What an unlikely spot for a Baptist preacher!

Though fired upon from all sides, Finlator stood his grounds. Defending himself in the *Christian Century*, he maintained that the policy articulated by the ACLU was exactly the Baptist interpretation.

> I know enough about the ACLU, conscientious objectors, humanists (secular and otherwise) and even Mrs. O'Hair to assert that all of them would strongly defend and support Baptists and others in their right to preach and practice these principles. . . . Because we have exchanged church-state separation for civil religion, we see only an enemy in the ACLU when it opposes the practice of prayer and the teaching of creationism in the public schools. . . . We Baptists should be the very first to recognize friends and allies, rather than foes and detractors in them, for upon my soul, there is absolutely no threat from these quarters, but only the strongest and most affirmative support for those basic fundamental beliefs we say we espouse. . . . I feel strongly about

---

[4]Ibid.

these assertions because of my personal experience. As a member and vice-president of the ACLU, I trace my civil libertarian convictions to my commitment to early Baptist principles, and I am confident that my involvement in the ACLU has made me desire to become an authentic Baptist.[5]

Finlator would be the first to grant that the boundary between church and state is always in doubt, and absolute separation is impossible. The goal is to coexist in mutual health and to preserve unfettered religious liberty. It is not always clear how to discriminate between the realms and to apply the principle correctly. The meaning of the enigmatic saying of Jesus, "Render unto Caesar the things that are Caesar's, and unto God the things that are God's," has long been debated. Within the ACLU Finlator had established the reputation of being a stickler for the fine points. A purist, he consistently pressed for the most meticulous observance. Accordingly, he found himself labeled an "extremist" on the subject by both civil libertarians and the religious zealots. In 1969 he defined himself as "more liberal than the ACLU."[6]

If some members of the ACLU thought him too liberal, one can imagine how he was received among Southern Baptists and other conservative religious bodies that, in their progressive acculturalization to American civil values, regarded the United States as *the* Christian nation and implored the government to enforce their conservative morality. His fellow Baptists seemed to have the most trouble following his line of reasoning. They joined him in opposing a diplomatic representative to the Vatican or allocating federal funds for parochial schools. But when he was enthusiastic about the Supreme Court ban on prayer in the public schools (1963), they divided sharply. One year their conventions would approve the ruling, the next year they would retract. When he moved to advocate the abolition of tax exemption on church properties, nearly all thought he had become too rigid and too doctrinaire. Leading the way in a policy debate on this question within

---

[5]Finlator, "They're Trying to Make Us Baptists," *Christian Century* 100 (6 April 1983): 303.

[6]Quoted in *Durham* (NC) *Herald,* 24 April 1969, 23.

his Pullen congregation on 4 May 1974, he urged paying the local taxes, which amounted to $20,000. In 1978, he managed to get a resolution passed by the Baptist State Convention that authorized a study of the problem. The study, "The Church and Tax Exemption," was presented to the 1979 Convention. His resolution read:

> Whereas, the vote in California for Proposition Thirteen has galvanized throughout the nation a radical reassessment of the issue of property taxation, and
>
> Whereas, vast and extensive properties, much of which are owned by church bodies, are exempt from taxation [and] which are coming increasingly under public scrutiny and
>
> Whereas, history unfolds dark pages of expropriation of such properties when the church has fattened on land and holdings, and
>
> Whereas: Baptists, while possessing extensive tax exempt properties, along with Catholics, Jews and Protestants, have nonetheless borne special witness through the years to the principle of church-state separation and have taken alarm at any infringement thereof,
>
> Now Therefore Be It Resolved that the Baptist State Convention of North Carolina, meeting in Raleigh, November 13-15 of 1978, make a study in light of the above considerations, of church tax exemption and advise the churches of findings and recommendations preparatory for further consideration at the next Convention.

Little interest was expressed in Finlator's resolution and the study it produced; his proposals, so principled and right in his own mind, lay buried in convention proceedings.

Finlator had not always been so sure of his position, nor had he always adhered strictly to the interpretation he forged for himself over the years. Nor were the lines he drew always so clear to others. For instance, in a 1942 article, he heartily endorsed using the public schools to teach religion. "Let us open up the Scriptures to our public school youth," he wrote, "and let us ground their secular education in the great fundamentals of the Hebrew-Christian ethic. . . . We must take the Bible into the public

schools."[7] He actually taught some of these classes himself. Forty
years later, when he was fighting to keep creationism from being
taught in the public schools, he reflected on the error of his ways.
"I do remember that I supported, raised money for and even taught
what must have been 'released time' classes in Bible in the local
Weldon High School. Angels and ministers of grace, defend me
from such folly!"

Moreover, where the Baptist hospital was involved and his
own alma mater had the opportunity to receive state and federal
funds, Finlator tended to go along. The landmark decision for
North Carolina Baptists occurred when they accepted federal
funds for the Wake Forest University medical school hospital in
Winston-Salem. Under the patriotism fired by the war and the
vision of dying soldiers without adequate medical care, the Baptists surrendered their hitherto "insurmountable" wall of separation. The dispute reared its head again, in 1978, with the
promise of federal funds to construct a biology research laboratory on the Wake Forest campus. Finlator sided with accepting
the grant, in a widely published article first appearing in the
Winston-Salem Journal.

> It would be helpful to keep in mind that an educational in-
> stitution created by a church body, however dear and deep the
> ties, is not the church on the campus, and certainly not an exten-
> sion of the church. By its very nature an educational institution
> is a separate and autonomous entity. . . . To understand this is
> basic. With regard to the matter of church-state separation, it is
> one thing for an educational institution with strong spiritual af-
> finities to a church body to accept federal funds to expand a bi-
> ology department. For the First Baptist Church to accept federal
> funds to build a parking lot for Sunday worshipers is another
> thing.[8]

Yet within five years of that concession, Finlator was argu-
ing, at the request of the *Biblical Recorder,* that tuition aid to

---

[7]Finlator, "The Bible and the Schools," *Biblical Recorder* 108 (5 August 1942):
7.

[8]Finlator, "Dear Old Wake Forest," *Winston-Salem* (NC) *Journal,* 19 February 1978, C3.

church-related colleges from state funds was wrong. For instance, for the academic year 1981-82 the seven Baptist colleges
in the state received $4,455,000 from the Convention and
$6,244,550 from the state. In Finlator's opinion they should re-
fuse all of the tax monies.

> With state support exceeding church support the question
> emerges as to when these institutions of higher learning cease to
> be church schools and in fact become state schools, and what
> might be done, or should be done, to preserve the continuing im-
> age of church schools. . . . It is when this right [to teach its own
> theological and moral views and to practice them] runs afoul of
> the government that the issue is joined. If the church school trims
> its theological sails to retain government funding, do we not then
> have to ask what is there unique about church schools? . . . Some
> of us must confess to deep doubts as to whether the church schools
> can retain their identity as church schools under ever increasing
> subsidies of the state.[9]

The evidence seems to indicate that Finlator was more wor-
ried about religious encroachment on the principle than the political. All his life he had observed overzealous religious moralists
foisting the "laws of God" on the civic order—laws against con-
traceptives, abortion and equal rights for women, laws against
acceptance of homosexuals and provision of social services to the
poor, laws favoring capital punishment and prohibiting alcohol,
drugs and sex education. Instead, he argued that the Christian
responsibility is to remove such laws from the statute books. In a
speech on "A Free Church in a Free Society," on 23 April 1967,
he challenged his audience. "I ask you, whether it might be wise
for the church to take the lead now, and before others do, in asking the removal of such laws on the books [that exist] for the
church, of the church, and by the church."

Finlator had grown up with so-called "blue laws," and with
prohibition. In fact, because of the churches, particularly the
Baptists, the "dry" laws endured in the South long after the Eigh-
teenth Amendment was rescinded. He had also witnessed the

---

[9]Finlator, "Debating Tuition Grants," *Biblical Recorder* 149 (11 June 1983):
3.

churches pressuring legislatures to enact laws forbidding the
teaching of evolution in the biology classrooms. When segregation in the public schools was given its death-knell by the 1954
Supreme Court decision, he saw these same Christians devise so-
called "Christian academies," using more often than not facilities of local Baptist churches. Therefore, with the appearance of
the Moral Majority campaigns in the 1980s, he had had ample experience with the religious encroachments upon the separation
principle. Moral Majority advocates demanded laws to enforce
their own moral standards; they wanted the courts to interpret
laws in their favor; they pressured the executive branch to side
with them.

At the Los Angeles Baptist Convention of 1981, Finlator took
them on; this time he won. The Convention adopted his resolution opposing, as the *Atlanta Constitution* reported, "interference
in religion by the government and interference in government by
religious groups." The *Detroit News,* on 13 June, described Finlator's resolution as "a move aimed squarely at the Moral Majority. . . . The criticism is bound to be a blow to the Moral Majority
which counts many of the 13 million Southern Baptists among its
members." According to the *Los Angeles Register,* the Baptists
"criticize the growing movement of the religious right; their motion appeared to strike at the tactics of the right-wing groups."

Finlator's resolution was hardly sensational; it was nothing
more than he had supported throughout his mature years. Only
this time it hit its mark. The time was ripe. At his urging, the
Convention resolved:

> That the Southern Baptist Convention, in accordance with
> and in commitment to the First Amendment to the Constitution
> of the United States, and to the historic Baptist principle of
> Church and State separation, deplore and reject the arrogation
> of the right of any group to define and pronounce for all people
> what is the Christian faith, and to seek through political means
> to impose this faith upon the American people under a govern-
> ment which is mandated to safeguard and respect the people of
> all religions and no religion.

Finlator had outfoxed the advocates of religious control of the state. But it turned out to be a Pyrrhic victory, for within a year, at its meeting in New Orleans, the Southern Baptist Convention approved prayers and the teaching of creationism in public schools.

Proponents of the religious right from all over the nation judged Finlator as their principal Baptist opponent. They bombarded him with letters. Typical are two that appeared in the Raleigh *News and Observer* immediately following the 1981 convention.

> The Rev. W. W. Finlator seems to think that Christians should be jolly good sports and look the other way while the forces of evil are wrecking our country and our children.
>
> I would remind him that the divine founder of our faith did not sit back and wring his hands when he saw evil against his children. He took a whip and threatened those who would vulgarize the decent and holy. He expects his followers to put up the same battle.
>
> To fight evil is not to "impose" our views on others. The situation has become an emergency. We are trying to prevent our beloved land from becoming another Sodom. And how about the atheistic, humanistic views that have been "imposed" on us, against everything we believe?
>
> I find it extremely difficult to understand how a God-called, Bible-believing pastor, dedicated to the principle of Judaeo-Christian ethic, would have such difficulty endorsing the principles of the Moral Majority or in making a distinction between the church and the Moral Majority. Nor do I think the Moral Majority is trying to take Washington or Raleigh or any other city for Jesus. However, those of us who are trying to reach this nation for Christ through the local church would certainly appreciate a little help or at least a little less criticism. Our conduct and involvement as private citizens in an effort to exercise our rights and responsibilities as Americans are certainly just as legitimate as the rights of those involved in the ACLU.

Finlator's critics hit the mark when they accused him of being the role model for preachers interfering in civil affairs. What they missed was the distinction Finlator tried to make between the tendency to move toward theocracy, on the one hand, and the struggle to humanize the political order with the ethic of Jesus, on the other. Those Christians seeking to legislate their own special brand of morality in order to make America a "Christian" nation with the messianic goal of ridding the world of "atheistic" communism did not seem to fit the latter category. From Finlator's point of view nothing could be more damaging to democracy and to Christianity than the blending of the American Way and of Christ's Way in a trivialized, blurred rendering of civil religion.

> Under a regime of civil religion the line between patriotism and religion tends to fade and our faith in God and our commitment to our country becomes the same. This is the basic danger of civil religion. It is immortalized in the lines from the national anthem which read
> *Then conquer we must, for our cause is just,*
> *And this be our motto: In God be our trust.*
> The true separation of church and state demands that there will be occasions when the church must protest vehemently against what the state does. Under civil religion God sanctions whatever Caesar proposes.

In an article, "Caesar and God," which he penned for a national journal in June 1981, Finlator saw the trend toward civil religion as

> an ominous moment in the history of the nation. . . . The church in so sanctioning the state has not only forsaken its witness, but has rendered a disservice to the nation: America is deprived of a conscience. . . . America began as a religiously neutral nation. Caesar and God had separate domains by official edict. . . . Today, however, the separation principle is for the first time under a potent, sustained and, I fear, orchestrated attack.

The coalition of political forces profiting from an alliance with the religious right, both of which would make short shrift of the Bill of Rights in their move to appropriate power, privilege and wealth, alarmed Finlator. He cited Lincoln as normative. While admitting that Lincoln did indeed speak of "this nation under God," he contended,

Those of the "moral majority" persuasion [take this to mean] that since our nation is already Christian, whatever it does is with God's approval and under God's protection. Not so Lincoln. He had spoken of the visitation of God's punishment upon our country for its wrongs. And here he was reminding us that a nation under God is a nation under the judgement of God. This is profound separation of church and state.[10]

To an accommodated civil religion the authentic church should take a prophetic stance, Finlator argued.

To a nation committed to militarism, the church must say: "They that live by the sword shall die by the sword." To a nation that condemns to benign neglect the powerless, the subculture, and the "nobodies," the church must say: "Inasmuch as ye did it not unto the least of these my brethren, ye did it not unto me." To a nation that supports the wealthy in their haste to heap up more wealth, the church must say: "Woe unto them that join house to house and field to field." And to a nation that regards its vast resources as an expression of divine reward for good conduct, the church must say: "From those unto whom much has been given, much will be required." Here lies true, honest-to-God separation of church and state. Only within this separation can we say the nation is blessed.[11]

On this prophetic distinction hinged Finlator's condemnation of the Moral Majority's political goals.

The fundamentalists are content to be repressive on their own theological and biblical issues. The Moral Majority has taken it a step further. They try to define the Christian faith politically. For them what makes a Christian are his views on abortion, homosexuality, prayer in the public schools, ERA or busing.[12]

Other than the prophetic stance of his Christian faith, Finlator relied mostly on his conception of the Bill of Rights. He dared to label the Bill of Rights "sacrosanct," as sacrosanct as the Sermon on the Mount. In doing so, he opened himself to the very

---

[10]Finlator, "Caesar and God," *Churchman* (June-July 1981): 12.
[11]Ibid.
[12]Ibid., 13.

charge of civil religion which he abjured. He could hardly deny
his single-minded championship of it. Writing to a friend about a
lecture he had given, he reported, "My entire talk was built
around the Constitution and the Bill of Rights which I 'bran-
dished' during my lecture like Billy Graham uses the Bible."
Again, answering a request in 1971 to contribute a chapter to a
book specifically devoted to Baptists and the First Ten Amend-
ments, he informed its editor, "The Bill of Rights is therefore very,
very precious to me and should be indeed to all Baptists. We would
hope that one of the good things to come out of this source book
would be the reconversion of Baptists to the spirit and letter of
the Bill of Rights in the American Constitution." As if to test Finlator's devotion to the Bill of Rights, the editor assigned him the
provision farthest removed from Finlator's forte—namely, the
amendment on the right to own property. Finlator took the challenge and promptly proceeded to build his case entirely on the
thesis that the intent of the amendment was to limit the owner-
ship and use of private property wherever property rights come
into conflict with human rights.

> There are no property rights as such. How can a lifeless thing
> called property have rights! Only persons have rights. . . . It may
> be instructive at this point to consider the proposition held by
> many that in our American system of government property is the
> keystone of all rights. Once again the Bill of Rights does not sup-
> port this view. The rights it declares are human rights. . . . Prop-
> erty is certainly not given priority in this particular amendment.
> . . . It must be noted that life and liberty precede property. . . .
> Nothing could be more helpful or healing to our country today
> than the recovery of an understanding that the Bill of Rights val-
> ues property but allows regulations or expropriation of property
> for the public good.[13]

Finlator's posture does appear ambivalent. On the one hand,
he vigorously battled those who would impose Christianity and
their conception of its morality on America; on the other hand, he
was inclined to elevate the determinative documents of Ameri-

---

[13]Finlator, "The Right to Property," in John Baker, ed., *Religious Liberty and
the Bill of Rights* (Washington: Baptist Joint Committee, 1972) 53-54.

can government and its democratic dream to the level of divine inspiration. Certain assumptions apparent in his political thought lend support to the charge that he had his own version of civil religion: that democracy is the best form of government, that Christianization of society leads to democracy, that the people can ultimately be counted upon to decide rightly, that the Bill of Rights has an absolute and an abiding worth. These are his civil norms. Yet, just as integral to his political philosophy was his contention that the autonomy of the secular state does have its limits, that humanity is incapable of perfecting a heaven-on-earth, that there must be prophetic judgment on the state, that there must be a "wall of separation" between the state and the church, and that in exercising one's political influence one acts as a citizen and not as an agent of the church. These tenets clearly point away from a civil religion.

Even when Finlator tended to equate the American Bill of Rights with the voice of God for America—*vox populi, vox dei*—he contended that there would be no Bill of Rights without the inspired contributions of his own Baptist forebears. The Bill of Rights did not drop from heaven, in Sinai fashion. American Christians must bring self-judgment upon their formulation and vigilance to their enforcement. "Civil liberties are never nailed down and fastened. Victories have to be won and rewon. It takes vigilance, and there now seems to be a slacking of vigilance," is the way the *Raleigh Times* reported him on 31 December 1983.

Finlator had the most trouble with the separation principle when his devotion to civil liberties came into conflict with his Christian compassion. For instance, organizations such as the Ku Klux Klan and Christian academies were diametrically opposite to him. Both groups used the cross to camouflage racism; yet Finlator came to the defense of their rights as citizens. Speaking to the Johnston County Humanities Forum in March 1978, he audaciously took on the hotly disputed local question about whether the Klan had a right to advertise on a roadside billboard. He not only approved that, but also its right to march. He had taken this position many times before, notably before the House Un-American Activities Committee on 11 February 1966.

I am prepared to go with [Representative Lennon] all the way
in safeguarding the civil rights of the members of the KKK for
the simple reason that they are all American citizens and entitled thereby to all the rights and privileges of citizenship. No
committee of Congress, famous for its quasi-judicial side shows,
has the right to discredit publicly and without due process the
members of the Klan.

He stood by this position even when liberal cohorts both within
the ACLU and certain Christian assemblies sought from the government extraordinary measures to restrain "disruptive" elements in American society.

In this country one has the right to believe and espouse unpopular causes. That right has to be defended, even for the Klan
and for the Nazi Party. Unless we defend the rights of people who
take positions we abhor as well as positions we support, our Bill
of Rights is futile. When it comes to safeguarding freedoms we
just cannot pick and choose *whose* freedoms.

Finlator stood by the Christian academies in 1978 when government procedures within North Carolina seemed to bring un-
due pressures upon their operation. In an article in the Raleigh
News and Observer, he reminded his readers that

these fundamentalist Christian schools are a legacy of certain
legislative deliberations designed to defy the Supreme Court ruling. . . . [But] let us back the fundamentalist churches in their
right to have their schools and day care centers. Their rights must
be honored.

While strongly insisting that no infringement must be made upon
religious practices, Finlator limited the state's right to setting up
"standards and regulations for the total welfare of the children."[14]
        The razor's edge Finlator walked as a citizen loyal to democ-
racy's highest ideals and as a Christian whose love embraced the
whole wide world, especially the hurt, was well-nigh impossible.

---

[14]Finlator, "What Say North Carolina Church Bodies on Religious Issues?"
News and Observer (Raleigh NC), 17 September 1978, 8.

The way he reconciled the two was not by regarding himself as a flaming liberal, as so many contemporaries tended to see him, but as a traditionalist harking back to authentic roots, as a Puritan praising and practicing the virtues of plain living, high thinking and hard work, and as a patriot relying on the founding ideals. Likewise, in his religious faith, he relished the primitivism implicit in the Baptist appeal to "the New Testament pattern." Finlator understood Jesus and the early church to have introduced a radically new way of relating to worldly power. While spiritual citizenship takes precedence over political citizenship, the Christian never obviates, forfeits, or surrenders his political responsibilities.

Within the ambiguity of patriotism Finlator pressed for the mature version. "There are, in my judgment, basically two Americas, one of the Star Spangled Banner and one of America the Beautiful, one that speaks of power and might and victory and the other that speaks of love and justice and beauty and self-control and compassion. It is the patriotism of the second America that I want emphasized."

Finlator's appeal to Puritanism inhered in his prophetic love for the primitive simplicity of life. In the Duke Chapel on 11 July 1976, he called for a recovery of this spirit.

> As much as I believe in a more equitable distribution of the national wealth, in social and economic justice, and in the bringing of all people under the protection of the Bill of Rights, I do not think that our nation has a future apart from some kind of revival in our private hearts of this spirit of Puritanism.

In an earlier sermon in the same pulpit on 19 August 1973, he had tried to disarm his critics. "I am definitely myself an institutionalist, perhaps an establishmentarian. I am truly a devotee of history and tradition and heritage." Quite conscious of the heuristic effect these catchwords might have, Finlator nonetheless took them seriously. For instance, before the North Carolina Judiciary Committee on 22 May 1975, he appealed to its members. "We are in fact strict constructionists—that the Constitution means what it says in its safeguards of freedom of speech and freedom of press." He did, of course, infuse labels like constructionist, institutionalist, traditionalist, Puritan and conservative with meaning derived from his own experience and philosophy. He did so in part to defuse those who might dismiss him as a far-out liberal or radical. But primarily he did so because he felt that he was basically adhering to the mainstream of the democratic tradition and to the central orthodoxy of the Christian faith.

To keep the two spheres neatly apart when human life in its foibles and idiosyncracies and ambitions defies such a dichotomy is an impossible task. To mold the two into one, whether under totalitarian statism or religious theocracy, is patently evil. To form a society where human rights and the Gospel converge is utopian. Ours is a nation where a compromise has been attempted, but where much agony of choice has been expended when the two spheres infringe and the citizen must make an ultimate choice. Finlator, in giving his life to pondering the intermingling of the two spheres, may have shed some light on the path of all who think it important and fruitful to agonize over that choice.

Chapter Seven

CHOOSING BETWEEN AMOS AND ERASMUS

THROUGHOUT HIS CAREER Finlator was torn between Amos and Erasmus, the prophet's condemnatory stance founded on a gloom and doom scenario over against the humanist ever hopeful in embracing the future for all of mankind. His first regular literary productions were signed with the pseudonym "Festus Erasmus," a series begun in the *Biblical Recorder* in 1940. These pieces appeared frequently until June 1944; during one six-month period he produced twenty-one weekly columns. Under the Erasmus byline the essays imitated both the style and the mood of the great humanist. In them he sought to apply the irony, the humor, the classical learning and the universality of Erasmus to the contemporary American scene, in particular to North Carolina and the things pertaining to Baptists.

Forty years later Finlator still felt obliged to come to the defense of humanism. This time he was answering the attack upon "secular humanism" launched by the new religious right, as expressed by members of the Moral Majority and the United States Senator from North Carolina, Jesse Helms, a fellow Baptist. On 9 August 1981 he delivered a sermon to his Pullen congregation that was widely reproduced in the press and appeared as an article in the *Churchman,* in December 1981. In it humanism found its locus in the Roman Stoics, in the Erasmian branch of the Reformation, and in the "secular state" concept of the founders of America. Finlator saw no conflict between these and Christianity.

During the same years Finlator struggled with the call to prophecy. Two more contrasting models by which to mold one's life are hard to find: Erasmus, the gentle compromiser, eager to mend divisions within the unity of *corpus Christianum* and to stand with time-honored institutions; Amos, the fire-brand from the backwoods, demanding instant purity, thundering his condemnation of evil, especially of corruption in high places, and pleading for the poor who were so ruthlessly abused. "Reform or be doomed," was the traditional prophetic message. Finlator, by nature, belonged to the gentleness and conservatism of Erasmus; he sought to bring out the best in all persons, to appeal to their sweet reasonableness, and to believe that the best is yet to be. Still he was tempted by the mantle of Elijah. *Also I heard the voice of the Lord saying, and who will go for us?* And what must the prophet prophesy? *Ah sinful nation, a people laden with iniquity, a seed of evildoers, children that are corrupters: they have all forsaken the Lord. . . . Wash you, make you clean, put away the evil of your doings from before mine eyes, cease to do evil, learn to do well, seek justice, relieve the oppressed, judge the fatherless, plead for the widow.* Whether Finlator fully comprehended the awful contrast between the measured forbearance of Erasmus and the rasping demands of the prophetic voice is open to question; that he attempted to combine them within one personality was a heroic venture.

There are signs in his first literary offerings that he did waver between Erasmus and Amos. While his very first column was entitled "The Poets Have It," and others subsequently concentrated on literary entertainment and inspiration, he was meanwhile publishing polemical pieces in the same journal. One of the first of these prefigured the dichotomy facing Finlator. It identified Jesus as a prophet with a defiant spirit. "It is for us to observe that wherever this spirit of defiance and daring has entered into the heart of man the stream of human history has changed its course."[1]

For the remainder of his life, Finlator would be torn between polar vocations: whether to play the role of Erasmus or the role of Amos. Logically and historically they are irreconcilable. To mix them is almost impossible. One role is irenic, the other bombastic; one persuades by reason, the other commands "thus sayeth the Lord"; one locates itself in the richness of human culture, the other where God dwells.

Finlator dreamed of bringing the two together in one personality. Trouble is bound to brew, however, because the tendency of the prophetic is to repulse, while the humanistic tends to attract. The prophet stands alone in the end, offending even his admirers, rejected by the world. The humanist cultivates a following; he must have imitators so that, after all, humanity will survive. Over the years Finlator moved in and out of the respective roles, not with the greatest of ease nor always sure that the public grasped which role he was playing.

The third verse of a sonnet composed by a member of Pullen to celebrate his retirement captures something of Finlator's prophetic stance.

> *The Prophet, often out in front of peer*
> *And congregation, gladly bore the scorn*
> *Of those who chose to neither see nor hear*
> *A revolution waiting to be born.*

But the sonnet's concluding couplet sees the dilemma.

> *A tow'ring ego, humble mein; in all,*
> *Enigma. Comrade, but in no one's thrall.*

Some credit for Finlator's dilemma may be charged to the Southern culture in which he was reared. It nourished both the

---

[1]W. W. Finlator, "Challenging Axioms," *Biblical Recorder* 105 (June 1939): 5.

classical humanist ideal typified—God forbid—in its Grecian
plantation architecture and its slavery base; it also gave birth to
the people's church, Baptists, with the democracy of the marginal
people, denied any entitlement in the "high culture." Finlator was
a child of both, yet he imagined that authentic Christianity could
purify and redeem both. His Southern Baptist culture cherished
the notion of prophecy without appreciating its full biblical aus-
terity. The likelihood is that he, so thoroughly immersed in the
bifocal culture, became fascinated with the sobriquet "prophet"
long before he grasped its radical implications. He has revealed
that he did not encounter the phrase "prophetic ministry" until
he was a sophomore in college. Instantly, he claims, he embraced
it as his own role. He pursued his seminary training in an institution that boasted of being "the best school for prophets" in the
nation. Yet he came to feel some embarrassment as he heard the
word celebrated and the prophet-heroes of the past eulogized but
observed that the professors and their protégés comfortably ex-
ited through the same door by which they had entered. It dawned
upon him that in their minds prophecy could be easily reconciled
with rapid social climbing until they occupied a county-seat pulpit, fitted out in a business suit not unlike any of the town fathers.

Finlator vowed he would be different. Being different, he later
explicitly outlined, meant focusing on those aspects of the Gospel
that have to do with earthly and social realities rather than with
soul-salvation for the next life or with devotional palliatives for
this life. In his first Erasmus column, he had written: "Enough of
'On Jordan's Stormy Banks' and the 'wishful eye,' and let us rise
to the challenging strains of 'Awake, My Soul, Stretch Every
Nerve, and Press with Vigor On.'" In a subsequent column, a few
weeks later, he declared, "Now I have always been fascinated with
the desire to be original." For him, this meant reinterpreting the
prophetic message for the twentieth century, specifically within
the small town environs of Eastern North Carolina (he was writing from his first pastorate at Pittsboro). In this novel self-assignment, he had no immediate models. He would have to hammer
it out for himself.

Looking back at that initial decision, he evaluated that moment in a sermon in the Duke University's Chapel on 11 July 1976.

> In this summoning up of remembrance of things past, I am impressed with the consistency with which I have fulfilled a commitment made years ago, which was that my ministry should give major emphasis to corporate and collective ethics rather than to private and individual morality. Not that I have minimized the latter at all but that I have long known that some 95% of my fellow clergymen would be working that side of the street to the neglect, as I feared, of what St. Paul called the principalities and powers and spiritual wickedness in the high places. Or, to borrow from Reinhold Niebuhr's great book, *Moral Man and Immoral Society,* my decision was to leave "moral man" to the tender mercies of my brethren while I, however ineffectively in my Don Quixote role, would take on the "immoral society," and I have no apologies.

His initial decision may not have been as clear or as easy as it appeared in retrospect. In that early day as soon as he diverged from the customary Sunday morning homily and commented upon the power ploys current in the local community, he ran into hot water. One community leader pulled him aside and warned, "Young man, you have the talent to put you at the top. My advice to you is to lay off such matters and quit meddling. Just stick to the Bible and you'll go a long ways." Finlator promptly ignored that advice and aligned himself with those few prophetic voices he detected within the fold of North Carolina Baptists, persons such as E. McNeil Poteat, Walt N. Johnson, and S. L. Morgan.

Morgan, already in retirement, had gained the reputation of being a maverick among Baptist preachers. He addressed a single sentence on a postcard to the young Finlator: "We need a prophet." In time he urged Finlator and a small coterie of liberal Baptists to establish the journal *Christian Frontiers,* which began in 1946. Later when Finlator publicly challenged the manner in which the three top Baptist Student Union executives were dismissed by the state convention in 1954, Morgan commended him.

This is just to say your article showed a chastened wisdom and
capacity to blaze a trail for Baptists beyond any other public ut-
terance I've read in a long time. Your sober reflections and doubts
and efforts to see the way out of present difficulties indicate you
have a perspective and a grasp of essentials, that, if held to, will
win for you a place of trusted leadership in our Baptist host. I hail
you as such a leader-in-the-making.

Significantly, the first article Finlator placed in a national
journal was entitled "The Prophetic Ministry." Much of its sub-
stance, though couched in the third person, may be taken as his
own painting of the prophetic portrait.

Today, as then, the prophetic ministry is the strait gate and
the narrow way, and few there be that enter in thereat. The demands are stringent, the requirements tough, and the journey
lonely. In every way the minister who chooses it is tasked and
challenged far beyond his brethren who travel highways sur-
veyed by tradition and paved with orthodoxy.

He proceeded to list five traits of the prophet necessary for contemporary times. One, knowledge of the Bible. Two, study of eco-
nomics, sociology, finance, politics, race relations, labor-
management and family life. "There is no place among the
prophets for undocumented passion." Three, courage. "Alas, the
larger fields through some mysterious divinity are under control
of the regular clergy where theology of 'God of things as they are'
makes them more acceptable to the powers that be in the economic order." Four, superiority to the conventional preacher as a
pastor. "The prophet must beware lest anyone dub him a social
reformer, period!" Five, an unimpeachable character. "He must
realize without one tinge of the martyr complex and with a good
pinch of humor and challenge, that they are all out to 'get' him:
his brethren in the ministry; his irate, privileged member; a con-
trolled chain press; some outraged representative of a veterans
group; the Chamber of Commerce; or the D.A.R." He quoted with
approval an unknown source: "If the church cannot produce
prophets to warn and lead the people, then she will produce priests
to read her own burial service."[2]

---

[2]Finlator, "The Prophetic Ministry," *Crozer Seminary Quarterly* 29 (January 1952): 39-43.

Finlator's embodiment of the prophetic in subsequent years is prefigured in this early theoretical formulation. With four of the traits he managed very well, but as the fifth, sensitivity to being called "a social reformer," he chafed the rest of his life. While Finlator knew that certain scholars interpreted the prophets of the Bible as social reformers, he strangely did not relish this label for himself. Yet this aspect of Finlator's behavior is precisely what the press continuously revealed. Years later, lecturing at Southeastern Seminary on 25 March 1976, he issued a warning to the students.

> The point I wish to make here is that we need not get ourselves tagged as a liberal or a radical preacher, or a do-gooder, or an activist, or even, if we moved from an adjoining county, an "outside agitator." Neither do we have to act like a martyr looking for a cause or rush out, as someone put it, to mount our steed and ride off in all directions. Our parishioners are by and large traditionalists and when they hear something coming compellingly out of the Bible, or from their authentic past, and interpreted in the light of the living present, they tend to hear it, and in part to accept it, even when it shakes them up, without turning against the faithful pastor who has also been the faithful scholar.

Perhaps Finlator was subconsciously confronting his own predicament, for some members of his own congregation were seriously doubting his ability to walk the razor's edge between being a good pastor and a social reformer. After all, the biblical evidence is weighted: the prophet is stoned. "That light is come into the world, and men loved darkness rather than light" (John 3:19). Finlator aimed to avoid what he knew in his heart was prophetic destiny. Despite his idealistic side, fortified with his humanist philosophy, he was ever conscious of the Achilles heel—truth thwarted by the hardness of human hearts. As Harrison Salisbury summed up the wisdom of his days, "There are no ends to which power will not go to put out its eyes."

Wary as he was of prophecy restricted to the narrow base of social reform, Finlator was cognizant of the larger problem attendant in presuming to be a prophet. In daring to wear the prophetic mantle, Finlator had to acknowledge he had taken on a task too large for himself or any other person.

> I once heard the famous Niebuhr declare that any man who proclaims today "Thus saith the Lord" is either a fool, a charlatan, or a prophet. . . . I have been all three of these. I may have called myself a prophet but I'm afraid I don't measure up. A prophet is one who fearlessly hears and fearlessly proclaims what he believes is the word of God. It is indeed presumptuous to make such a claim.

But there was nothing to prevent others who admired Finlator from applying this esteemed title to him. Especially was this true of fellow ministers within his own denomination who were inspired by his courageous example. From dozens of letters received over the years that affirmed his prophetic image, I quote two.

> Thank you for being prophetic when very few church people are willing to take the risk. Whether you know it or not you are a sign person in my pilgrimage. It is never easy to be a prophet but your thoughts were relevant and very prophetic. I personally struggle to maintain this kind of integrity in my ministry and find it difficult to always be an honest prophet.

> It is always an inspiration to know creative, prophetic ministers. It is especially inspiring and encouraging to find them among our Baptist ranks. How I wish there were many more like you.

Finlator smarted under this attribution, a label thrust on him by others, a label he did not deny. If a prophet is defined as a person possessing an extraordinary moral sensitivity and a passionate commitment to social justice, then Finlator was not far removed. But, as we have seen, he took pains to clarify that to be prophetic is to be *more*. The prophetic vocation demands superhuman powers. It expresses itself in the ecstatic, a stance beyond the world. It entails an abnormal quality. A person cannot choose to be prophetic; God designates the prophet. That person then announces God's destruction of the commonplace, God's shaping of history. The prophet's judgment, his call to repentance, and his specified change in habits all may eventuate in social reform. But the two forms are not to be mistaken. In Finlator's case, the evidence indicates he conformed more to the social reformer side. In replying to an admirer on 5 June 1974, he wrote, "You couldn't say a nicer thing than refer to my efforts as possessing "a prophetic ring" because that is exactly what I would like to aim at but so often lack the courage and commitment to achieve."

Throughout his life the tension between the harsh aspects of prophecy and the good sense of the common man, between the unpredictable proposals of the prophet and the solid social realism of the humanist, between the anti-institutionalism of the prophet and the culturally enriching goals of the humanist would plague Finlator. He was by nature and temperament tenderhearted and compassionate; to hurt someone's feelings would be his last wish. As he stated repeatedly, he favored the traditional and supported conventional institutions. Still he was intrigued by Karl Barth's famous dictum that: "Religion must die. In God we are rid of it. . . . Now the prophetic *crisis* means the bringing of the final observable human possibility of religion within that scope of the Kingdom under which all human endeavor is ended." Prophecy as outlined by Finlator followed this Barthian radicalism.

> As I see prophecy it reads: in compassion God speaks to the human community through prophets. Those who authentically represent God have interpreted the activity of God in social history. They answer the presence of God in the midst of political and economic life; they foretell the judgement and hope that are implicit in the loyalties and practices of the common life; they set forth the vision of the covenantal renewal. . . . Yes, I have always wanted to be a prophet. I think of the minister as a prophet. The ministry must be all of this; otherwise it can really be a sort of cop-out and a desire to escape from the awesome and shaking prophetic word.

Sometimes his prophetic ardor burst the bounds of homiletic nicety. A journalist friend who heard him one Sunday morning wrote to applaud and to remind him of his recklessness. "You must have had a hearty breakfast Sunday since you took on the U. S. foreign policy, missionaries, Southeastern Seminary, haters, literalists, fundies, all at once in a single thirty-minute round. Old Diogenes would have parked his lamp outside Pullen on that day."

Pricking the conscience of his generation was Finaltor's principal prophetic achievement. That he succeeded in this self-assignment is seldom argued. President Ralph Scales characterized Finlator, when his alma mater awarded him an honorary doctorate in 1973, as "the state's gadfly." A newsman summed up his life as one who "piqued the patience" of the South. Indeed, on many occasions, he was less than diplomatic in choosing the time, the place and the person to be challenged "in the name of God." His victims sometimes felt that he was enjoying himself at their expense. Finlator saw it differently: when public wrong was flagrant it was no time to stay silent. Floyd McKissick, the black civil rights lawyer who often worked alongside Finlator, compared him to Amos, dropping his plumbline beside a crooked generation. Finlator was self-conscious of this side of "God's wild man." He conceded the point in writing his close friend, Dr. Glenn Archer, on 5 September 1967.

> Dr. W. L. Poteat, who was once the distinguished president of Wake Forest College, used to say that if a man in love did not indicate some sort of mental aberration he doubted if the young man were really in love. I should like to plead guilty to being "off" in some of the commitments that are dear to my heart. . . . You are right: "anybody who is a crusader is partially crazy anyway."

With the popular notion of prophecy as prediction Finlator had little to do. Nonetheless he was appreciated by many for being far-sighted, perceiving things ahead of his generation. Gerald White, a lawyer who heard Finlator in the Elizabeth City congregation after the Supreme Court desegregation ruling in May 1954, recalls "the prophet Finlator reminded us that laws are to be created and interpreted in terms of social justice." Finlator had no patience with the kind of prophecy marketed by the electronic church, in which God is locked into fanciful timetables, calculated from a peculiar reading of limited scriptural passages, and is coming soon to destroy the planet earth. Finlator's conception rested on the Hebrew word for "turning," the call to return (repent) to the ancient path of divine law and to the eternal order of justice.

During one particularly stressful period, when Finlator was under severe attack in the public press, Dr. Warren Carr, pastor on the Wake Forest University campus, published a public letter in his defense. "Bill Finlator," Dr. Carr wrote, "takes the Christian ethic so seriously that he offends many people. Paraphrasing I Corinthians 1:23, he scandalizes some and is foolish in the view of others. In short, he is a prophet! I confess that I cannot explain him."[3]

Prophecy is rare because it originates in the particularity of divine revelation. Humanism has a broad base; it draws upon the universal human spirit. Humanism elicits everyone's contribution to establish a coalition in order to save mankind. The human response to prophecy is colored by disbelief, shock, fear, misunderstanding, and finally disobedience. Therefore the ultimate word of prophecy is good news, that of God's grace. Any tension contingent upon the polarity of these two ways of viewing reality finds some resolution in the last statement. Prophecy and humanism are in fact about the same business: the recovery of humanity and the preservation of the good earth. At least something like this undergirds Finlator's enthusiasm for humanism.

"As far as calling myself Erasmus, I did," Finlator recalls.

It was a bit sophomoric and I was trying to combine the word Festus, which of course is a Roman name in the New Testament and which means joy, to Erasmus which stands for wisdom and humanism. Still I truly would like to identify myself. with much of what goes under the banner of humanism. Somewhere I have read that Martin Luther wrote about Jesus that "if we take hold of Him as a man we would discover that he is God." Most of His teaching and action in the New Testament was mundane, that is to say, having to do with human life.

For a lifetime Finlator embraced the causes humanists embraced. And from his side he battled what he took to be a false dichotomy, Christian versus humanist. But within the conser-

---

[3]Warren Carr, Letter to Editor, *Biblical Recorder* 135 (24 May 1969): 10.

vative Southern Baptist Convention, the controversy would not go away. In the 1970s and 1980s the conservative religious attack reached national proportions. Finlator mustered his energies in rebuttal, publishing numerous articles and finally taking the floor of the Southern Baptist Convention convening in Los Angeles in the summer of 1981 to introduce a resolution to stem the tide. It actually passed!

"We have a controversy which in my judgment is unnecessary, unfortunate, and avoidable," Finlator declared in a major speech on 5 February 1980.

> A deep love-respect should, even if in some cases it doesn't, exist between the Christian and the Humanist. A willingness to listen and understand and work together would resolve many differences. And both have a shared and paramount mutual concern which in religious terms is the salvation and redemption, and in humanist terms is the enrichment and fulfillment, of our common humanity.

Even so, Finlator, schooled from his many years of confrontation with fundamentalism, was fully cognizant that adherents of the new religious right were no more ready to welcome Erasmus than they were Amos. Dress up humanism, take away its "secular" modifier, give it a converted status, it would still be offensive to them. The very concept strikes at the sectarianism, the sectionalism, the anti-intellectualism, the crusading militarism of a Christianity in captivity to culture. "I would not like to be known as a Christian humanist," Finlator says.

> The phrase is redundant. To be a Christian is to be a humanist in the highest and fullest and best sense. That's the crux of the Christian message. Christ was a humanist, the perfect humanist. Therefore I don't mind being called a humanist. I am a Christian who is also a humanist. It is a beautiful word. No one can truly believe in the doctrine of incarnation and reject humanism. "The word became flesh and dwelt among us." Or, again, "God so loved the world."

In a 1981 article in *The Churchman,* Finlator complained that "two beautiful words, 'secular' and 'humanism,' expressive of so much historical content when used singly, have been put to-

gether and made to sound diabolical and subversive." He charged
that Christian fundamentalists "have saddled together [these two
words] with an effect that is little short of blasphemous." He suspected a more deep-seated basis for popular religion's opposition
to humanism: it exposes the coalition of religious sanction and
political and economic exploitation. The God-elected few are
blessed with power and privilege in this life and with heaven in
the next. Such an interpretation of the doctrine of election, he felt,
undermines the full nature of the Christian message.

> Christians have always been afraid of this total humanity of
> Jesus and what it implies. It is a terrible threat to man's inhu-
> manity to man. We therefore prefer to keep this Jesus mystical,
> divine and distant. And yet the church through the centuries,
> while affirming the divinity of Jesus, has pronounced the denial
> of His humanity a heresy. . . . The Christian faith for all its mys-
> tical and transcendent and supernatural qualities is yet the most
> materialistic and humanistic religion on earth. The doctrine of
> the incarnation is God's ultimate affirmation of the good earth
> and the sacredness of humanity.

Finlator felt that Christians, instead of shunning and denouncing humanists, should join hands with them in common
cause. From his own experience, engaged in endless hours in
heady sessions with a plethora of interest groups, to regard humanists as enemies of the faith was ridiculous. "There aren't that
many humanists around to get uptight over!" was his standard
retort to the witchhunters. He had watched these "good pagans"
busy serving humanity, often shaming believers in their zeal for
righteousness. In a celebrated 1978 sermon, "Why I Joined Them,"
he pointed out that "the smaller groups particularly are unselfish, that they exist for the cause of others, that we could write over
each of them the Latin phrase 'pro humanitate.' " On another occasion, referring to the anticapital punishment group, he celebrated "the ethical fervor, and even moral outrage, and yearning
for human dignity, which motivates them. This moral passion is
an element that must be retained." These struggling, feeble protest bodies identified with minorities—backing lost causes, siding with the poor and the outcast—Finlator labeled "the valiant

hearted." In their company he found his sagging spirit, buffeted by the defeats that had been administered to him by official religion, renewed. The playwright Paul Green, the statesman Frank Porter Graham, the civil rights lawyer Marion Wright, the editor Tom Lassiter, the labor organizer James Dumbrowski, Ann and Carl Braden, Benjamin Mays and Floyd McKissick, to name only a few, were humanist allies in many a cause. When the churches seemed ashamed of Finlator, such humanists rallied to his side. In an editorial in *The Smithfield Herald,* on 4 May 1973, Tom Lassiter called Finlator "the true humanist."

This should not imply that the persons listed were alien to the church. That alienation was less likely to happen in the South than in other parts of the nation. The humanists Finlator associated with may have been in revolt against religion's hypocrisy but they did not renounce their spiritual heritage, the very heritage that shared with Finlator. In a 1954 letter to Finlator, one of these friends, after registering his long love-hate affair with the Baptists, confided,

> I wish I were a part of a church in which we were free to seek Christian truth. I believe in soul-competency and soul-freedom. I don't believe I have any truth or convictions if what I have is imposed upon me by somebody else, preacher or layman. The church stifles my spirit and reduces me to a cog in a machine when it tells me I must believe black is white while my own light, dim as it may be, tells me white is white.

Working so frequently alongside humanists, Finlator may have been prone to favor them indiscriminately. His tendency was to give everyone the benefit of the doubt. In a lecture to the Watauga Club, "Christians and Humanists," on 5 February, 1980, he generously characterized humanists.

> The humanist would find himself in general agreement with the affirmation of our humanity in Christ. The humanist is a person who believes if not in the perfectibility of homo sapiens at least in his endless improvement and growth, and is committed to the eradication of injustice, inequity, poverty, suppression, ignorance and whatever else [may] impede the realization of the full potential in every human being. . . . The humanist does thank

whatever gods, or whatever destiny, there be for entrusting him with the courage and the vision and the ability to remold his life and his world nearer the heart's desire.

It may be that Finlator, so anxious to appreciate the good, the beautiful and the true within every person, slid over the time-honored philosophical and theological distinctions between Christians and humanists. Where other Christians had reservations, Finlator could proclaim with abandon, "Many, many Christians hold the same views as humanists—I for one." Yet it is clear from his own personal experience and from his continued proclamation of the Christian faith that he was intimately and vitally aware of the difference in the gods being honored.

Finlator devoted his life to reducing the tension between the humanist and the prophet. For him they were ultimately and fundamentally the same. The God of the prophet was forever disclosing the true humanity of creation and of the revealed law. The honest humanist was forever obliged to come to grips with the God within. Yet the question remains, for Finlator as it did for Pascal, is the God of the Bible the same as the divinity of man? Is the God of Abraham, Isaac and Jacob to be equated with the divine spark within human flesh? No one investigating Finlator's career doubts that within his own soul he confronted the living, transcendent God into whose hands it is a terrible thing to fall. Those who knew him, in all his brassiness, all his showmanship, all his biased loyalties, also knew that for him God took precedent over every other consideration. His humanism derived from the fact that his God could not separate from nor abandon any human being.

ESSAYS AND ARTICLES
BY WILLIAM WALLACE FINLATOR

Biblical Recorder

"Religion in Life" (4 May 1938): 4.

"Can Justification Be Sin?" (15 June 1938): 1.

"The Christian Must Instruct His Conscience" (17 August 1938): 1.

"The Peril of Pulpit Freedom" (30 November 1938): 4.

"Challenging Axioms" (7 June 1939): 5.

"Not Depraved, But Irreverent" (13 September 1939): 11.

"Lessons from a Piano Concert" (3 January 1940): 11-12.

"Festus Erasmus" [FE], "The Poets Have It" (15 May 1940): 6.

FE, "On Building Fences" (22 May 1940): 6-7.

FE, "Primal Sources" (29 May 1940): 7.

FE, "Do You Know It by Heart?" (5 June 1940): 7-8.

FE, "Shall I Draw You a Picture?" (12 June 1940): 6.

FE, "On Growing Old" (19 June 1940): 5-6.

"The Importance of Knowing How to Hate" (3 July 1940): 12-14.

FE, "If We Neglect So Great a Flattery" (3 July 1940): 6-7.

FE, "Suspended Animation" (10 July 1940): 6-7.

FE, "What's in a Name?" (17 July 1940): 7.

FE, "They Rub You the Wrong Way" (24 July 1940): 6-7.

FE, "Speaking with the Tongues of Men and Angels," (7 August 1940): 7-8.

FE, "Lest We Remember" (14 August 1940): 5-6.

"Safeguarding Our Baptist Democracy" (21 August 1940): 6.

FE, "A Pair of Fresh Eyes" (28 August 1940): 5-6.

FE, "Unsafety in Numbers" (11 September 1940): 5-6.

FE, "The Art of Saying Nothing" (25 September 1940): 6.

FE, "Rediscovery of Reading" (9 October 1940): 6.

FE, "Fun in Being Natural" (16 October 1940): 6.

FE, "Reductio ad Personam" (30 October 1940): 6.

FE, "Untouched by Solemn Thought" (13 November 1940): 5-6.

FE, "The Long and the Short of It" (27 November 1940): 5.

FE, "Defense of Cosmetics" (11 December 1940): 6.

FE, "Welcome, Second Childhood!" (8 January 1941): 7.

FE, "Exploiting Your Opponent" (15 January 1941): 6-7.

FE, "The High and Holy Use of Humor" (29 January 1941): 6-7.

FE, "Imagine Yourself a Christian" (12 February 1941): 6.

FE, "When Earth Is Sweeter Green" (26 February 1941): 5.

FE, "Armed with a Song" (12 March 1941): 5.

FE, "Redemptive Altercations" (26 March 1941): 5.

FE, "Writing Yourself Full" (16 April 1941): 5-6.

FE, "Rejuvenescence of the Commonplace" (7 May 1941): 5-6.

FE, "For Love's Sake Only" (21 May 1941): 5-6.

FE, "Prophets Without Hearers" (4 June 1941): 5.

FE, "Preaching to God's Chillun" (11 June 1941): 5.

FE, "Teachers Without Certificates" (6 August 1941): 5.

"Do We Know Too Much about Ourselves?" (20 August 1941): 9-11.

FE, "Out of the Mouths" (27 August 1941): 5.

FE, "The Art of Receiving Praise" (24 September 1941): 5.

FE, "Truth and Tact" (22 October 1941): 5-6.

FE, "Are You a Two-Timer Too?" (21 January 1942): 5-6.

FE, "Door Bell Ringers" (28 January 1942): 5-6.

FE, "It Has Been Said Before" (4 February 1942): 6.

FE, "In Debt to Our Children's Children" (11 February 1942): 5-6.

FE, "Too Zealous to Be Courteous" (18 February 1942): 5-6.

FE, "Ritual in Their Faces" (11 March 1942): 5-6.

"All Out Defense" (1 April 1942): 8-10.

"This Is Not Armageddon" (17 June 1942): 10-11.

"The Bible and the Schools" (5 August 1942): 7-8.

"I.O.U. Happiness" (28 July 1943): 10.

FE, "Scouring the Anchor" (12 January 1944): 10-11.

FE, "Show Me First Your Penny" (26 January 1944): 10.

"Pastors and Prejudice" (15 March 1944): 7-9.

FE, "Dearly Movie-Made Beloved" (29 March 1944): 10-11.

FE, "Alchemy in Reverse" (7 June 1944): 6.

"Let Protestants Be Protestants" (14 March 1945): 4-5.

"Southern Baptist Centennial and the New South" (15 August 1945): 6.

"There Are Church Conventions and Church Conventions" (17 July 1946): 4.

"What Think Ye of Christ?" (19 October 1949): 4.

"The Pink People Called Methodists" (10 June 1950): 4.

"This I Do Believe" (5 August 1950): 5.

"The Book Nobody Plugs" (28 October 1950): 8.

"To Leave So Many Worthiest Books Unread" (6 January 1951): 9.

"Whose Bride Is the Church?" (29 March 1952): 2.

"How to Keep the Smear from Sticking" (30 August 1952): 6.

"Naked and Ye Clothed Me" (30 December 1952): 7.

"Let's Have No Fellowship with the Censor" (18 July 1953): 2.

"Town and Gown" (column, 13 June 1953-11 September 1954).

"Testament of Doubt" (27 March 1954): 2.

"A Southern Baptist at Evanston" (23 October 1954): 6.

"Baptists Are on Record" (15 October 1955): 6.

"Four Areas of Concern" (7 November 1959): 12-13.

"The Baptist Image" (12 December 1964): 7.

"The Right to Be Heard" (21 May 1970): 11.

"The Graham Plan" (7 April 1973): 7.

"Debating Tuition Grants" (11 June 1983): 3.

"Give to Us Peace" (12 January 1985): 3.

Churchman

"An American Tragedy" (June 1967): 3.

"The Post Office and Religion" (January 1968): 6.

"Tribute to GES" (August-September 1969): 7.

"How to Get Along with Black People" (April 1972): 3.

"Nuremberg and Vietnam: An American Tragedy" (December 1972): 3-4.

"A Plea for Amnesty" (April 1973): 5.

"I'll Skip Billy Graham" (October 1973): 3-4.

"Kickoff Without Prayer" (October 1974): 7.

"Young in Spirit" (November 1974): 3.

"Theology behind Poverty" (March 1975): 6.

"The UN: A Necessity" (October 1976): 7.

"Why I Am a Conservative" (November 1976): 6.

"Baptist in the White House" (February 1977): 5.

"America's Good Life: Home, Church, Family" (May 1977): 3-4.

"Not So Fine Carolina" (July 1979): 9.

"Caesar and God" (June-July 1981): 12-13.

"Civil Liberties in North Carolina" (October 1981): 6-7.

"Creationism and Thomas Huxley" (December 1982): 10-11.

"Jesus Was a Humanist" (October 1984): 9.

"Why I am a Secular Humanist" (January 1985): 13.

Other Publications

Editorials. *Christian Frontiers* (January 1946-January 1949).

"Better Late than Never, But." *Young People* (May-June 1950): 2-3.

"The Pink People Called Methodists." *North Carolina Christian Advocate* (22 June 1950): 2.

"Liberty, Equality, Justice." *Reveille* 12 (January 1951): 1.

"The Prophetic Ministry." *Crozer Seminary Quarterly* 29 (January 1952): 39-43.

"Whose Bride Is the Church?" *Prophetic Religion* 9 (Summer 1952): 3.

"Let's Have No Fellowship with the Censors." *Baptist New Mexican* (16 July 1953): 7.

"A Church with a Chancel." *Review and Expositor* 52 (October 1955): 11.

"Prayer for Jefferson-Jackson Day." *Congressional Record* 103, 4 (1 April 1957): S 4909.

"Until Our Churches Repent of This Denial." *News and Observer* (Raleigh NC), 25 October 1959, 8.

"Build on Aycock's Dream." *Goldsboro* (NC) *News,* 10 November 1959, 6.

"What's Right, What's Wrong with North Carolina." *News and Observer* (Raleigh NC), 27 March 1960, 10.

"Christ in Congress." *Congressional Record* 108, 5 (11 April 1962): S 6282.

"Rights and Responsibilities of Southern Labor." *Charlotte* (NC) *Observer,* 5 May 1962, 12.

"The Christian Amendment." *Liberty* (May 1963): 1.

"Mr. Baptist, Meet Mr. Catholic." *North Carolina Catholic* (October 1963): 1.

"New South Emerging." *Charlotte* (NC) *Observer,* 7 May 1965, 8.

"A New Look at Labor." *Charlotte* (NC) *Observer,* 6 September 1965, 8.

"World Peace, A Spiritual Imperative." *Pulpit* 37 (November 1966): 4-7.

"An American Tragedy." *Congressional Record* 113,3 (20 February 1967): S 4026-28.

Letter to Editor. *Charity and Children* (30 November 1967): 7.

"Letter to Meany." *North Carolina Labor News* (October 1969): 1.

"Political Duty Is Religious." *Winson-Salem* (NC) *News,* 18 January 1970, 1-4.

"Free Indeed." *Charity and Children* 83 (May 1970): 1-2.

"The Right to Be Heard," *Arkansas Baptist* (21 May 1970): 4.

"Please Don't Call It Christian!" *Baptist Program* (June 1970): 7-8.

"The Right to Property." In *Religious Liberty and the Bill of Rights,* John Baker, ed., 53-55. Washington: Baptist Joint Committee, 1972.

"A Motorist's Prayer." *Raleigh* (NC) *Times,* 23 August 1974, 12.

"A Short Sermon." *U.S. Farm News* (July 1975).

"I Am a Conservative." *News and Observer* (Raleigh NC), 29 August 1976, 3F.

"N. C. Branded No. 1 in Suppression." *Asheville* (NC) *Citizen,* 4 September 1976, 4.

"Sir Walter Raleigh." *News and Observer* (Raleigh NC), 12 December 1976, IV:3.

"A Letter to Jimmy Carter." *Charlotte* (NC) *Observer,* 1 January 1977, 11.

"Address to New Americans." *Congressional Record* 123, 12 (11 May 1977): S 1431.

"Dear Old Wake Forest." *Winston-Salem* (NC) *Journal,* 19 February 1978, 6.

"In the Catbird Seat." *Winston-Salem* (NC) *Journal,* 16 July 1978, 8.

"What Say North Carolina Church Bodies on Religious Issues?" *News and Observer* (Raleigh NC), 17 September 1978, 8.

"Unsporting to Labor." *Report from the Capital* 35 (August 1980): 7.

"Two Eminent Preachers Engage in Debate." *Sandhills Citizen* (Aberdeen NC), 10 December 1980, 2.

"Economic Justice and Religious Community." *Fair Measure* 4 (March 1981): 2, 4.

"The Right Hand of Fellowship." *Christian Ministry* 12 (July 1981): 15-16.

"Today's Code Words Distort Truth." *News and Observer* (Raleigh NC), 27 August 1981, 5.

"Memories of a Grand and Awful Time." *Winston-Salem* (NC) *Journal,* 30 July 1982, 8.

"Marching to the Promised Land." *News and Observer* (Raleigh NC), 19 October 1982, 10.

"They're Trying to Make Us Baptists." *Christian Century* 100 (6 April 1983): 303.

"A Time to Oppose Modern Herods." *News and Observer* (Raleigh NC), 23 September 1984, 5.

"The Ministry and Economic Justice." *Review and Expositor* 81 (Spring 1984): 245-48.

"The Moment of Decision Has Come." *News and Observer* (Raleigh NC), 23 September 1984, 5.

"A Look at the Politics of Morality." *Winston-Salem* (NC) *Sentinel,* 8 February 1985, 10.

INDEX OF NAMES

INDEX OF SUBJECTS